D0810436

Caught in the Conflict

MY LIFE WITH JAMES WATT

by Leilani Watt
with Al Janssen

HARVEST HOUSE PUBLISHERS
Eugene, Oregon 97402

Caught in the Conflict

Copyright © 1984 by Harvest House Publishers
Eugene, Oregon 97402
First printing, March 1984

Library of Congress Catalog Card Number 83-82700
ISBN 0-89081-411-2

Printed in the United States of America.

DEDICATION

To those who may think of
themselves as mere wives,
but who are, in fact, women of destiny.

ACKNOWLEDGMENTS

It is no small task to plan and supervise the metamorphosis of a woman from what she is to what she must become. I want to acknowledge that it was when God asked the most difficult commitments from me that He also gave me the most help to begin the process. During these years my husband, James, has held me through the tough places, and has encouraged me to be all I was meant to be.

Of our friends in the Reagan Administration, Don and Barbara Hodel have shared the most intimately in our past three Cabinet years. It was Barbara's comment at our kitchen sink that started this whole project.

While many others have strengthened us during our stay in Washington, Sallie Clingman committed herself to walk with me through valleys of conflict and on peaks of courage. It was quite a hike!

To Al Janssen belongs special acknowledgment. His ministry is to help others tell their stories; without his determined purpose this book could never have been written. I am especially grateful to Al and to Harvest House for encouraging me to write.

However, two special friends deserve my recognition. Our two children watched me struggle with pain and conflict, and yet they believed with me that I would win. To Erin and to Eric, and to their loved ones, I can recommend these same answers—as well as to others who find themselves caught in the conflict.

—Leilani Watt

CONTENTS

CHAPTER ONE

THE BEACH BOYS

The familiar shaky feeling and now-hesitant speech made me admit I had waited too long for the antigen treatment. I leaned back in the waiting room chair at Dr. Brodsky's office. What a welcome sound the classical music was, yet I could not totally relax. Although my eyes were closed, my mind was on the alert for a news flash. I had heard of Al Haig's sudden resignation as Secretary of State last year while in a doctor's office. Now I listened beyond the beauty of the radio music for an interruption which would announce another political casualty.

After the antigen treatment the fog lifted from my mind. How grateful I was for this new medical breakthrough after years of searching! By evening I would be renewed and eager to attend another round of receptions as a Cabinet member's wife.

As I started out the door, I practically collided with another patient coming into the office. Her friendly face was familiar from previous visits, but I did not know her name. "I just saw your husband on television!" she said, full of enthusiasm. "He was holding the cutest little foot!"

My mind tried vainly to recall if James had told me he would be on television that morning. But to be polite, I answered, "Really! I wonder what that's all about?"

"Well, it had something to do with the fact that he's going to invite the Beach Boys back for the Fourth of July."

Those words hit me like a truck. I felt the blood rush from my face, leaving me weak. With a polite statement that I'd see it on the evening news, I rushed out to my car. An early afternoon shower had passed, and the April sun had warmed the vinyl seats of my cream-white Horizon. I leaned back and let the heat soak into my shaken body. *That can't be true,* I thought. *My husband has never changed a decision that he knows is right. Patriotic music on the Fourth of July is right. What happened? One more media flap might be the last straw, and he will be out of office.*

I need to calm down and get some information. I flipped on the radio, already set to an all-news station. The top-of-the-hour news broadcast had started, but nothing was said about my husband as the announcer finished the national and local news roundup and moved into a brief sports report.

I started the car and slowly began the ten-minute drive home, while twirling the radio dial to find another news report. Finally, back on the all-news station, I heard it: "Interior Secretary James Watt appeared at the White House today to apologize to First Lady Nancy Reagan," said the plain-voiced announcer. "In a meeting afterward with the press, Secretary Watt appeared with a bronzed hole-in-the-foot award that was presented to him by President Reagan. The Interior Secretary indicated that he would be glad to invite the Beach Boys back to Washington again."

My heart was pounding. *That didn't answer my question. Is James changing the program for this year's Fourth of July?* I drove into the parking space behind our townhouse, quickly locked the car, and headed into our home. I called Kittie, my husband's confidential secretary, and asked if I could talk to James. "He's in a meeting right now," she answered. "Do you want me to interrupt?"

Usually I said no, but this time I said, "Yes, for just a minute."

His voice came on the line almost immediately. "Hi, Lani, what's up?" (He almost never calls me Leilani; I always call him James.)

"I heard the news on the radio and wondered if everything was okay."

"Yes, I had a very interesting experience at the White House. I'll tell you about it when I get home." His businesslike voice was light and enthusiastic. There was nothing in his tone to indicate any serious problems— only that this was not the time to talk.

I was not reassured by his voice. After we hung up, I walked to our living room and nestled into the striped wingback chair by the patio. It was too early for the network television news reports, so I occupied my mind by recalling how this whole mess had erupted. Following the July Fourth celebration in 1982, a woman with the Washington chapter of Parents for Drug-Free Youth had complained to my husband about the use of drugs on the Washington Mall, a part of the National Park System. She had stated that Park police had arrested 40 adults among an estimated 418,000 for offenses such as disorderly conduct and assault during the festivities. Many of them were at a "smoke-in" by some 500 people who openly flouted the laws against marijuana. More than 600 people had been treated at medical facilities, many of them for drug-related problems.

As Secretary of the Interior, my husband was respon-

sible for managing all of the national parks in the United
States. While the use of drugs such as marijuana and
cocaine was strictly illegal in the park system, enforcement of the drug laws during a large festival involving
several hundred thousand people was virtually impossible. Police usually ignored any drug offense. Last year
many of those on drugs had disrupted others who simply
wanted to enjoy the entertainment. There were numerous reports of fights, broken glass, and thefts.

I remembered how my husband had considered the
various options available and had decided that the
simplest solution was to change the type of program offered. The rock bands seemed to draw a primarily
college-age crowd. He thought that having patriotic
music on the Fourth of July would encourage diversified
age groups to participate, making it more of a family
occasion. James had told me in November that he had
sent a directive to the Regional Director of the Park Service, saying, "It is imperative that. . . we get entertainment that will point to the glories of America in a patriotic
and inspirational way that will attract the family."

That had been nearly five months ago. Last week I
had sat in on an interview with a reporter from the *Washington Post.* James had talked about the Department's
involvement in the United States Holocaust Memorial
Council activities. He had also mentioned changes he
had made in the Department, including plans for the
Fourth. Yesterday's *Post* had reported this one aspect
of the interview in a front-page story, stating that James
had banned rock music from this year's Fourth of July
celebration because of his concern that it was attracting
"the wrong element." As background, the article
reported that in 1980 and 1981 the Beach Boys had
performed. In 1982 the Grass Roots were the featured
group. *The Grass Roots. Is anyone defending them?*

This year it had been arranged for Las Vegas singer

Wayne Newton and the U.S. Army Blues Band to perform. "We're trying to have an impact for wholesomeness," James was quoted in the *Post*. "July Fourth will be a [traditional ceremony] for the family and for solid, clean American lives. We're not going to encourage drug abuse and alcoholism, as was done in past years."

How could this story be misinterpreted to mean that my husband didn't like the Beach Boys? I thought. *Amazing! He never mentioned them, and they weren't even the performing band in 1982, when he made his decision! I know he based his decision on crowd control. There ought to be a broader cross section of people at this national celebration.*

I desperately tried to stop my mind. To pray. To be silent. Instead, I realized that all across the country newspapers and television and radio stations would come out with headlines: JAMES WATT BANS BEACH BOYS. The newscaster had reported that the local FM rock station was urging listeners to send letters and make calls to the White House, airing their feelings about Watt. Kittie had said the telephone operators at the Interior Department and the White House were swamped.

When we read this morning's paper, we knew we had trouble. Vice-President George Bush was reported as saying the Beach Boys were "my friends and I like their music." Mike Deaver, White House Deputy Chief of Staff, had said in a television interview, "Anyone who thinks the Beach Boys are hard rock would think Mantovani plays jazz." My husband looked at me after reading that quote and asked, "Who's Mantovani?" We laughed together at him and his humor. Then I wondered aloud, "Why *did* Mike make any comment on something you never said?"

What right do the media have to make up their own facts? Surely that can't be. So I reread the paper. Buried in a follow-up story by the *Post* was a quote by a Georgetown youth who had attended the '82 concert: "I love the Grass Roots, but the crowd was the biggest group of undesirables I'd ever seen. . . . There were people beating each other up. There was broken glass all over." This was the issue, and patriotic music was the solution. Instead the press hammered James and distorted his motivation.

Then what had happened at the White House? The clock was striking 7:00. I crossed the hall to our dining room and opened the doors of an antique oak washstand. My husband had refinished it to hold our television set. I leaned forward on the edge of a chair as the NBC anchorman, Roger Mudd, led off his evening report with the story: "The White House made clear today that, while it was willing to take on Congress and the Soviet Union, it would not take on the Beach Boys. From Ronald and Nancy Reagan on down, the White House climbed all over Interior Secretary James Watt today for his refusal to allow the Beach Boys to play at this year's Fourth of July celebration." *Refusal? They weren't even invited to come this year!* "As Robert Hagar reports, the Administration tried to make a joke of it."

Roger Hagar appeared on the screen with the White House in the background. "The Beach Boys, who've appeared on Washington's Mall for two of the last three Independence Days, will be invited back to appear on the Mall again, but not on July Fourth, a White House official says. This year's program, he said, is already set, with Wayne Newton."

As Hagar continued his report, film clips were shown of my husband, with his now nationally recognizable bald head, walking out of the White House into a light rain. He was smiling and holding a bronze foot with a hole in it. "This afternoon Interior Secretary Watt emerged from a meeting with the President," Hagar said, "and a telephone conversation with Mrs. Reagan to say the President had given him a bronzed fiberglass foot with a hole in it—the shoot-yourself-in-the-foot award."

The film then showed my husband talking: "And by the way, I've learned about the Beach Boys in the last 12 hours. And we'll look forward to having them here in Washington to entertain us again."

A reporter off-camera asked, "What was Mrs. Reagan's involvement?"

"She said that she is a fan of the Beach Boys and that her children had grown up with them, and they're fine, outstanding people and that there should be no intention to indicate that they cause problems."

Another reporter asked, "Do you plan to apologize to the Beach Boys now?"

"I don't know that I owe them an apology, but I apologize to anybody who thinks they need one."

As the report finished, I noted that James had *not* changed his decision. He had not said that there would be rock music this year. He was only saying that he had nothing to do with the Beach Boys' future schedule in Washington. *He is just bearing the brunt of this issue for the White House. My husband deserves an Oscar.* I switched channels. ABC was showing a clip of President Reagan joking, "I've just called in Ambassador Phil Habib to settle the Jim Watt/Beach Boy controversy." Sam Donaldson was in the middle of his report: "Given such supporters, it came as no surprise today when James Watt, displaying a new gift trophy, announced he'd changed his mind about the Beach Boys."

Donaldson concluded his jovial account by stating, "It may still be only Wayne Newton on the Mall this Fourth of July." *Only Wayne Newton? That insults him!* "It may be too late to get the Beach Boys there now. But never mind. They're welcome on the Mall anytime, according to James Watt, who's changed his mind about the Beach boys, with a little help from his friends."

Finally I flipped to the CBS Evening News. Dan

Rather quipped, "Turning now from foreign tennis and Ping-Pong diplomacy to domestic top 40 rama-lama-ding-dong diplomacy, Bruce Morton reports that, after a hard day's night, Interior Secretary James Watt is now singing a different tune. Rock and roll is here to stay and surf's up for the Beach Boys for an Independence Day concert on the Mall."

Mixed with clips of the Beach Boys, my husband was made to look foolish. *Humiliating. None of the reports is even asking why James made his decision in the first place.* Bruce Morton concluded his tongue-in-cheek report to Dan Rather by saying, "Next time, Mr. Secretary, you may want to try something easier, like taking on motherhood or apple pie." I felt like throwing the remote control unit through the TV screen. But as I flipped off the television, I knew I had to calm down before James got home. If he was relaxed about the controversy, it wouldn't help him for me to be upset. I walked into the kitchen to begin dinner.

Many evenings we had social obligations, so we preferred to eat lightly when we were home. Often we ate a simple meal of soup and salad. James walked in shortly after 7:30 and, as he usually does, joined me to help slice vegetables for the salad. Working in the kitchen helped him to relax after a long, pressure-filled day. When our food was set on the small round oak table in the dining room, James turned on the switch to a small lamp that backlit a parchment sign on top of an antique hutch. I had made the calligraphy for him shortly before he was named Secretary of the Interior. "Come to the Quiet" it read. He sat facing it, a nightly reminder that home was his refuge. A cassette recorder poured hymns into the background.

After a few sips of soup, James began to tell me what had taken place in the White House that morning. "Well, Craig Fuller [President Reagan's director of Cabinet affairs] called me aside after I had appeared with the President before a group visiting the White House. Craig said we need to 'get this behind us.' " That's the normal phrase used by Administration staff when an issue needs to be worked through quickly so it won't dominate media attention any longer. "Craig explained that Mrs. Reagan was very upset and wanted to talk to me. 'Where?' I asked, wondering if I was headed for her office. Craig said she was already waiting for me on his phone.

"In his office, as I picked up the receiver, I had an uneasy feeling. Mrs. Reagan came on the line, and I knew by the tone of her voice that she was angry. How, she wanted to know, could I have canceled a 20-year contract with the Beach Boys to perform on the Mall for the Fourth of July?"

I whistled. "What did you say?"

"I just listened. I knew this was no time to defend myself. The Beach Boys have never had a 20-year contract. I wondered how Mrs. Reagan could have gotten that information, but I just listened."

"But didn't you tell her about the Parents for Drug-Free Youth or—"

"No, I just listened. When she was finished, I said I'd see what I could do."

My napkin fell to the carpet as I dashed into the living room to retrieve the morning paper, and we scanned the article. There it was: "Over their 20-year career, the group has participated in many events. . . ." *Ah-h-h! Career, not contract.* James was remarking how easily that could have been misread, but I couldn't be as generous and folded the paper in dismay.

James was engrossed in buttering his roll, but I was waiting for more details. "As I put down the phone from Mrs. Reagan, I was told that I would have to apologize and invite the Beach Boys back. I was really disgusted by then. I let them know I was *not* going to apologize for my decision. I was *not* going to invite the Beach Boys to this year's Fourth of July celebration. I had already offered a contract to Wayne Newton and I was going to stand by it. Dave Gergen, Director of Communications, had joined us by then, and when the phone rang, he answered. I recognized Mike Deaver's voice, calling to see how things were going. 'It's not going well,' I yelled from across the room. 'You'd better get down here!' Mike was down in a minute, and the four of us discussed how to lay the issue to rest. I reviewed the facts: the drug problem on the Mall, my decision to have a family event and the patriotic music that day, and that I had never mentioned the Beach Boys in the *Post* interview. I told them bluntly that it upset me that the White House staff, instead of checking the facts when the media asked them for comments, had in fact agitated the situation."

After a few bites, James commented, "I'll have to say this, though. To the credit of the White House, this is the only time a negative comment on me has come out of there. They've been loyal."

His words stung. Avoiding my own thoughts, I prompted, "Where did the foot come from?"

"Oh, Gergen brought out a bronze-painted, plaster-cast foot with a big hole in it. We all laughed and I agreed it was a pretty good way to end this controversy. 'Now the President is waiting for you,' someone said. I asked, 'What's the President got to do with this?' Mike said, 'Take this foot up to him and he will present it to you.'

"Can you imagine such a trivial reason to interrupt the President? But I followed instructions and went up to the Oval Office, interrupting a luncheon meeting between the President and Vice-President. 'Mr. President, you're supposed to give me this foot . . . .' The photographer was there to catch the twinkle in the President's eyes as he said something about my being a good sport, and that the foot was a traveling trophy.

"I laughed with them and mentally prepared to return to my office with the foot, when I was told, 'The press is waiting for you.' I was dumbfounded at all this staging. 'What do you mean the press is waiting?' Mike said, 'We have the press corps standing right outside the White House. You're to go tell them the President gave you this shot-in-the-foot award. And be sure to tell them that Nancy Reagan likes the Beach Boys and that they will be welcomed back into town anytime they would like to come.'

"With the three presidential advisers, I walked to the door. I don't know how long the press had waited in the rain. As I went through the door, the others hung back, and I was left alone to handle the press. It wasn't as easy as it looked."

I reached across the table to touch his hand. Shaking my head in discouragement, I said, "Jamie, in my view, you won an Oscar today. You are wonderful."

That reminded him of one more thing. "Back in the White House after the show was over, Dave Gergen put his hand on my shoulder and said, 'You're a good sport, Jim!' I just kept on walking, and I said, 'I am not a good sport. I am a good soldier. I will do anything necessary to help Ronald Reagan.' Every man nodded."

After he finished his story, we both were quiet for a moment, and only the ticking of our clock and the quiet sound of our spoons dipping in the soup interrupted our thoughts. I felt drained. "You know what amazes me about all of this?" remarked my husband, looking up from his meal. "The whole thing was orchestrated. I was reminded today how easily you can be pushed out of office. They could have had a letter of resignation ready for me to sign, and I would have gone out to meet the press and announce that it was all over."

James leaned his head back into the Queen Anne chair. I knew that he was disturbed that he had again caused embarrassment to the President. Already he had been involved in more controversy than any other Interior Secretary in recent history. There had been heated battles with environmental groups and frequent demonstrations against him as he appeared around the country. The Sierra Club had collected more than one million signatures in an effort to force him from office. Some Indians had been offended by his statement that reservations were a perfect example of the failure of socialism. Some Jews had been offended when he wrote a letter to Israel's Ambassador to the United States, advocating Jewish support for Interior Department energy policies. Pro-abortion groups had been offended by his public stand against abortion. Any one of these controversies could have brought his term to an abrupt end.

This has not been all fun, has it, Jamie? I thought, identifying with how he must be feeling. *You came all the way to Washington because the President asked you. You mean it when you say you'll gladly step aside the moment your usefulness is over. But this—this is so wrong!* In my mind, I saw the hinged crystal plaque the President had given James as a Christmas gift: THERE IS NO LIMIT TO WHAT A MAN CAN DO...IF HE DOESN'T MIND WHO GETS THE CREDIT. *The reverse must also be true—if you don't care who gets the criticism.*

James saw himself as a servant, and servants serve at the pleasure of their master, without expecting any favors in return. We hoped this latest public humiliation would satisfy the media and put the matter to rest. That would allow the President to proceed with more important matters. I could tell that, as far as my husband was concerned, the issue was now closed.

But not for me. I was greatly agitated by the unfairness of it all. I felt that my husband had been betrayed. That night, while James lay sound asleep next to me, I stared around the dark bedroom, able to make out only the faint outlines of our dresser and the rack holding my husband's ties. To my right were two chairs, with his Bible laid open, ready to read in the morning. *How could those men know the facts and not say anything,* I fumed. *Just a simple word from the White House could have ended the controversy. And why didn't anyone tell Mrs. Reagan what my husband had actually said? After all, she is concerned about drug abuse. If she had only known what my husband was doing, she might have understood and supported him.*

I was desperate by now for peace of mind. And sleep. I prayed again for Mrs. Reagan and for Mike Deaver, hoping to fall asleep on a good note. Before I reached the edge of sleep, I realized I was rehearsing two speeches. For Mike Deaver, I had scathing words: *Mike, how could you do such a thing?* I would ask, controlling my anger, yet making sure he knew I was mad. *You knew the facts! You knew my husband never mentioned the Beach Boys. Why didn't you tell the press? You could have put an end to it. Instead you made my husband look foolish.* I sat up in bed, ashamed of indulging my anger.

However, tumbling behind it came a more gentle speech for Nancy Reagan. *Did you know that James never mentioned the Beach Boys in that interview?* I would tell her. *He was concerned about the drug problem on the Mall during the rock concerts. So he thought it would be good to have patriotic music and attract families to this national celebration.* In my mind, I saw Mrs. Reagan smiling in her gracious, understanding way, patting me on the arm and saying, *It's okay, Leilani. I understand now. Thank you for giving me that information.*

I shivered. I was wide awake, and I suddenly remembered that, in less than two weeks, I was going to have to face Mrs. Reagan in a receiving line. *I hate conflict—mine or anyone else's. These speeches are futile. They're not going to change this national whoop against James.* The dull ache that filled my chest swelled to my throat. As a

Christian woman, I had to settle my inner turmoil. I knew that the responsibility for resolving this belonged in my heart alone, since to everyone else it was a closed issue.

But why should my husband be left looking foolish? Woman-to-woman I needed at least to have Mrs. Reagan understand, to believe the best of James. Choking back hot tears, I snuggled up tight to James and finally slept. *Let's hope tomorrow will be better.*

Morning came too soon. After breakfast, as I handed James his briefcase, he commented on my restless night. "You've got to get this behind you, Babe. Mrs. Reagan was defending her husband, and I like that." He touched my chin tenderly and was out the door.

The snap of our heavy metal door brought a picture to my mind—a long hallway of closed doors. For nearly 40 years I had run from conflict. I had just shoved down resentment and bitter thoughts. I had refused to admit to anger. I had avoided people. I had avoided circumstances which might have hinted at pressure or conflict. That process had closed many doors in my life—to God, to James, to health. I began to clear away the breakfast dishes.

Recently I had learned an effective way to deal with conflict, but applying it today was like a contest. *Who will win?*

The sharp ring of the telephone made me jump. Turning quickly, I answered the phone, and as the minutes passed I became enthusiastic in the conversation. It was a welcome diversion, but as I hung up, my mind returned to last night's thoughts. Suddenly and clearly these words filled my mind: *Wait. It will be better than all your planning.*

Instant relief overflowed. I knew where those words came from. I knew, in part, that they meant God had a plan for our lives beyond what I could see. It would not be easy, but I would do just what I had heard. Wait.

Wait. It will be better than all your planning.

CHAPTER TWO

MY INAUGURAL CRISIS

The morning of the inauguration was gray and cold. The military limousine crept through snarled traffic into the city. Two military escorts, who were assigned to get us delivered to all the right places, looked sharp in their navy blue dress uniforms. They sat stiffly in the front seat while James tried to make conversation with them.

"Have you men been in the area long?"

"No, sir," said the driver. The other man didn't answer.

"Tell me about yourself. Are you married?"

"Yes, sir."

James looked at me and raised his eyebrows, as if to say this discussion had no future. I took advantage of the opportunity to ask, "Tell me again what our schedule is for today."

"Well, after the inauguration, we'll sit in a special box with the other Cabinet officers for the parade. Then I have a meeting, so these men will take you home. Then tonight, we have a candlelight dinner at the Kennedy Center. If we're still on our feet, we'll go to the inaugural ball."

The car pulled up in front of the Capitol. The two military escorts quickly jumped out and opened our doors. The wind cut right through my coat, so I knew James must be freezing without his. We hurried into the Capitol building behind our two escorts.

"Where are we headed?" James asked.

"To the holding room, sir." I was glad James finally asked the escorts to slow their pace for me. The room was one James knew well from previous Washington years.

Other Cabinet members were already enjoying the warmth of coffee in the high-ceilinged, walnut-paneled room. I could see the beginnings of team camaraderie. James introduced me to William French Smith (Attorney General) and his wife, Jean, plus the Weinbergers and the Meeses—all from California. Labor Secretary Ray Donovan and Cathy started an easy conversation with the Blocks and us. I was glad I had glanced at this morning's *Washington Post* article with photographs and descriptions of each Cabinet officer. *How will I ever remember all these names and positions?* Here were the Lewises and the Schweikers, who were from the same church in Pennsylvania. The Haigs surprised me. Mrs. Haig was like a delicate figurine, and for all the authority he would wield, I expected the Secretary of State to be a taller man.

As usual, James became engrossed in a conversation, so on my own I met Sofia Casey, whose eyes twinkled merrily, and Midge Baldrige, a tall redhead. They were enjoying Ann Edwards' easy Southern grace. I knew I would remember Ann Regan, wife of the Secretary of the Treasury; she had beautiful white hair. We women were such a variety! But today our men were identical, at least in their formal clothing. *Handsome as they are, they're going to freeze,* I thought. But the men didn't seem to notice, for January 20, 1981, was a historic day.

The excitement left me thirsty. I searched the Hepplewhite table beside the entry door for a pitcher of water. Seeing none, I asked a serene lady, who was Betty Ruth Bell, wife of the Education Secretary, if she had noticed any ice water. Together we asked a steward to bring four glasses of water, including two for our husbands.

One wife I hadn't met was walking away from the group. "If you're thinking of sitting down, you have the best idea," I said, introducing myself and joining her. Her husband was Sam Pierce, Secretary of Housing and Urban Development, and she was Barbara, a physician from New York. The few moments we shared touched my heart, and a dear friendship was begun.

We were interrupted by a man firmly directing us to form two lines as he read our names. Forever after at official Washington functions we and our husbands stood, walked, and sat according to this protocol. Later I learned that the protocol was determined by the year in which a particular department had been established. The Department of Interior was founded in 1849, ranking us fifth behind the Departments of State, Defense, Treasury, and the Attorney General.

At the last possible moment the steward appeared with the much-needed water. James, who despises lines, was off talking to Jeane Kirkpatrick, Ambassador to the United Nations, when our line moved through the heavy doors and out into the hallway. He caught up in the corridor and joined the line, giving me a "See, I made it!" glance. He could walk a tightrope between my need for assurance and his need for excitement. The line moved quickly now, and we were escorted through large wooden doors onto the inauguration platform.

It seemed like a dream to find myself here. The Washington Monument stood majestically against a pale, powder-blue sky as we looked out from our fourth row seats on the west side of the Capitol. Many of the 150,000 spectators were hidden below us by the podium, but I could see the edge of the crowd surrounding the statue of General Ulysses S. Grant and the great reflecting pool at the head of the Mall. Beyond them stretched a carpet of brown grass dividing the buildings of the Smithsonian Institution.

I noticed that the sun had burned away the light cloud cover, but the wind sharply offset any warmth. Some had commented that this was the warmest inaugural in recent history, but I folded in the lapels of my collarless wool coat to fight off the cold. To my right, my husband sat stiff and uncomfortable in a traditional morning suit that made him look more like a butler than the President-elect's fifth-ranking Cabinet officer. Like me, James was from the plains of Wyoming, and we had laughed earlier today about how he, an independent Westerner, had just lost his freedom. All week long he had been told where to be and when. He had quickly bought a tuxedo for all the formal events. He was particularly self-conscious in a chauffeur-driven limousine. To him it didn't make sense having someone open and close the car door when you were capable of doing it yourself.

As the U.S. Marine Band played "Battle Hymn of the Republic," James put his arm around me. As I looked up to meet his eyes, which were bright with awe, I thought back to the first time I'd seen James at the hardware store in Wheatland, a town of 2300 in southeast Wyoming. Actually, I'd noticed his father first— mustached and proper, dressed in a suit. Few men wore business suits in Wheatland; my father didn't own one. Mr. Watt was the new lawyer in town, and his wife, also dressed in a suit, was manager of the Globe Hotel. After inspecting this couple, I noticed their son, his face displaying a broad, toothy smile. He was tall for an eighth-grader, nearly six feet in height, with broad shoulders. He had a high forehead that was accentuated by thick glasses. His curly reddish-blond hair was brushed back. Unlike most of the guys, who wore blue jeans, he was dressed in light blue sailcloth slacks and a short-sleeved plaid shirt. Together, the three of them looked like a city family that I might have seen pictured in *Life* magazine.

Later I learned that the boy's name was James—not Jim or Jimmy. He always signed his name "James G. Watt," and my classmates pestered him to reveal what the "G" stood for. He would just smile and say, "Guess." I could still remember the first time I'd felt attracted to him. I was enjoying a soda in the drugstore with some of my friends when I heard him talking in the booth behind me about the fun he'd had that summer in church camp. Temporarily ignoring my girl friends, I peered over the tall wooden back to get a better look. I thought to myself, "That's the kind of boy I'd like to be around. He's a Christian."

Someone told me that James liked the color red. Though I disliked the color, I made a bright red gathered skirt with a wide waistband and a big bow in back, and I was wearing it one day in band class when he first noticed me. I saw him ask the boy next to him, "What's her name?" When the boy answered with my tongue-twister, "Leilani Bomgardner," they both started laughing. My face turned as red as my skirt, for my name had often been a source of teasing. My grandmother had named me after Bing Crosby's rendition of "Sweet Leilani, Heavenly Flower."

But James was a considerate boy, and it was easy to forgive him when he passed me a note in the hall

one day. It was signed "James Gaius Watt." Gaius!
Guess, pronounced with a Southern drawl. It had been
a clever clue. One look into his friendly brown eyes told
me that he hadn't revealed his middle name to anyone
else. It was his way of saying I was someone special.

I was the only girl James ever dated. I was always
cheering him as he competed in sports. We sat together
on band trips and sang in chorus. Together we won most
school honors, both local and state.

Our relationship was forged during long walks while
he shared his dreams. James wanted to do something
to change America and make it a better place to live.
His goal had been to become a United States Senator
from Wyoming. His strategy included attending the right
school—the University of Wyoming—getting to know
key business and political leaders in the state, and living a moral life above reproach. I was a good listener.
I didn't know or care much about politics, but James
Watt was a man I could follow. I felt secure with him,
and he was comfortable with me.

We went off to college and spent long hours study-
ing together in the library. We were married during our
sophomore year at the University of Wyoming. His pro-
posal was not made in a romantic setting, while watching a beautiful sunset or during a candlelight dinner. Instead it came casually, while we were on an errand for
his mother.

We walked out the kitchen door behind the Globe
Hotel where he lived, and he asked, "How would you
like to be married when you're 19?" It was then early
August, and my nineteenth birthday was less than three
weeks away. I liked the idea and suggested August 31,
since that was both our parents' anniversary. "No, I want
to live at the fraternity house first," he answered. He
explained that he had lived in the dorm as a fresh-
man pledge. He would like to say that he had been a

fraternity man, and that meant living at the house. He stood and thought for a minute. Marriage meant giving up any eventual fraternity leadership. He said, "I figure it will take two months to learn what it's like to live in a fraternity house." And so we were married on November 2, 1957. I wore a satin princess-line wedding dress, which I designed and made, and James wore a muted rust plaid suit that was a bit too large. Our honeymoon lasted one day—before we headed back to classes!

Within months it became evident that our personality differences were going to cause me acute discomfort. While we were dating, he had given me most of his attention. Now I began to see another side, particularly how forceful he was in political discussions. James was a driver, willing to push forward and make things happen, even if it made other people uncomfortable, whereas I never wanted to upset anyone. I could be supportive of people with totally opposite viewpoints, unwilling to take a stand. James was decisive, never looking back once he made a decision. I found it hard to make a decision if I felt someone might disapprove. He was sometimes dominating while trying to convince others of his position. I would never push my point of view for fear that other people wouldn't like me. James was never awed by anyone, though he had respect for authority. But I was overwhelmed by a strong personality. He was always able to see good in even the worst situations. He was optimistic, looking for any advantage in the midst of adversity. However, I was devastated by adversity, unable to see how any good could result from it. James was a risk-taker. I wanted to play it safe. He loved to tell a joke, especially making fun of himself. Sometimes he could tease a friend unmercifully. I shriveled under such kidding. To me it wasn't any fun at all. In fact, in all our years together, he had never treated me with anything but dignity and respect. Yet during discussions I feared he would demand tough responses from me as he did from others.

I hated conflict. James had always valued strong opinions, but I could not handle my own inner turmoil in disagreements. Our differences could easily have led to a stormy relationship. Instead, I retreated, thinking that I was pleasing him. With only a couple of exceptions, I surrendered to the force of his personality. My life became wrapped up in our two children and any pursuits that promised tranquility. Those were the activities that brought me fulfillment, without confrontation. I gave little affection to James and received even less emotional support from him.

A cold gust of wind broke my reverie. The Marine Band continued to play as the last of the dignitaries was seated. President and Mrs. Carter were being escorted to their seats, and the ceremony would begin shortly. I noticed that my husband was deep in thoughts of his own. His gaze seemed to be on a far-distant future. I thought about the very beginning of James' political career, which had taken shape by his being in the right place at the right time. In 1962, after finishing law school, he joined the campaign team of Governor Milward L. Simpson, who was running for a seat in the United States Senate. After a successful campaign, Senator Simpson invited James to be his legislative assistant. That had brought us to Washington for the first time, where for 15 years my husband had served the Senator, had lobbied for the Chamber of Commerce, and then had been appointed to various posts at the Department of the Interior. In 1975 President Ford had named him to the Federal Power Commission, and he had served there until President Carter abolished the Commission. In August of 1977 we had moved back west to Denver, where James became president of the Mountain States Legal Foundation.

For my husband, the nearly 20 years since college had been a steady climb up the political ladder. But during many of those years I was largely unaware of the significance of his success. Instead, I was wrapped up in my role as a parent and in searching for identity through various leadership activities. We were two people living together, but with little involvement in each other's lives. Only recently, while we were in Denver, had some dramatic changes occurred. My husband was so pleased with my new interest in his life that he had started calling me his new wife.

I thought of the years I had ignored politics. Now I was immersed in it—and thoroughly enjoying it! I still got goose bumps thinking about the phone call less than two months ago that had led to this historic moment. James' nomination as Secretary of the Interior was a complete surprise to the nation. He hadn't even been on the list of candidates for the position. But his years of experience in the Department, his compatibility with Reagan's conservative philosophy, and his tough personality made him well-qualified.

Environmental group leaders had voiced strong opposition to his nomination as soon as it was rumored, and again during Senate confirmation hearings. Wyoming Senator Alan Simpson, in recommending James for this position, had said, "This is a bear of a job, and it will take a grizzly to do it." For a moment all the tingling excitement of this historic moment drained from me. *What did that mean?* It was a question I had mulled over several times. Some people thought it was impossible to reconcile the congressionally-mandated responsibilities that included protecting the environment while developing the nation's natural resources.

My husband loved challenges. He was incredibly excited about this new job. But a grizzly? A grizzly was relentless. He stood his ground no matter what weapon was aimed at him. He charged ahead in the midst of danger if the goal was worth the risk. With me, James was gentle and caring. But this job required all the attributes of his hard-driving personality. I knew that his matter-of-fact manner, stating the facts without concern for the feelings of others, would probably cause problems. But now wasn't the time to dwell on that; I wanted to enjoy this ceremony.

With a fanfare from the U.S. Army Herald Trumpets, we all rose as President-elect Ronald Reagan came down the aisle with his wife, Nancy, who was dressed in a bright red coat and matching braid ring hat. The crowd went wild with cheering. On tiptoes I stretched to see the serene face of Mrs. Reagan, so calm at her husband's side. He was acknowledging guests and Cabinet members, shaking hands with those closest to the aisle. His cheeks were glowing with health and enthusiasm. The Reagans were seated to our right, four rows in front of us.

James and I held hands as the Marine baritone sang ". . . America, America, God shed His grace on thee." The Reverend Donn Moomaw gave the invocation, and George Bush was sworn in as Vice-President. Then Ronald Reagan, dressed in a charcoal-gray club coat, striped trousers, and dove-gray vest and tie, took the oath of office before Chief Justice Warren Burger. I shivered with excitement as our new President received a 21-gun salute and the band played "Hail to the Chief."

President Ronald Reagan stepped forward to make his inaugural address. "To a few of us here today, this is a solemn and most momentous occasion," he started in his now-familiar, breathy voice. "And yet, in the history of our nation it is a commonplace occurrence."

Suddenly I was overwhelmed with fear. *What will be expected of me as a Cabinet member's wife?* This morning, after the traditional service at St. John's Episcopal Church, another Cabinet member's wife had asked me which coat I was going to wear this evening. She was wearing cloth, and was considering fur for the inaugural ball. I realized that I didn't have a choice. This otter-colored wool coat was the only warm dress coat I had.

James and I had chosen to live a simple lifestyle. It was normal for us to be looking for a used car here in Washington. Now I felt out of place at this ostentatious celebration. I was embarrassed to think that the gown I had made for the inaugural ball was perhaps inadequate, but there wasn't time to shop for a more appropriate one. Besides, I wasn't sure what was appropriate. *What is a farmer's daughter doing among such wealthy business leaders and entertainment stars? Surely the other Cabinet officers and their wives are used to a more luxurious lifestyle, and fraternize regularly with dignitaries.* Until this week we had only been spectators. *Is who I am and what I've chosen good enough for Washington?*

My mind was jerked back to the farm—640 acres of absolutely flat, treeless land atop a sandstone bluff in southeast Wyoming. A few miles down the road from our house was a tiny community called Slater, which didn't even merit a dot on most maps. In order to purchase supplies or attend school, we had to drive 30 miles to Wheatland. The nearest children lived six miles away, so my older brother, Lyle, and I usually played together. In the summers we hiked, played war in the wheatfields, and shinnied up the sides of the two grain silos.

My father was a dry-land wheat farmer who had worked hard to make his farm productive in the midst of a hostile, dry environment. Summer dust storms sometimes dumped an inch or more of silt on the land. I thought of him now, undoubtedly watching this event on television. He was a tough, barrel-chested man who kept his deepest feelings to himself. My greatest satisfaction as a child came on those occasions when I had won a sewing award at the fair. He would puff out his chest, pound it with his fist in pride, and state, "That's my girl!"

My early years were spent working with my mother, helping fix meals for the family and farm help. I was responsible for milking the cows and feeding the chickens and pigs. Mother taught me all the basic skills a farm girl needs—plucking and cutting chickens, cooking, sewing, and interior decorating. She was a very creative woman who could take a plain, sparsely furnished room and turn it into a display worthy of a *Good Housekeeping* photo spread.

We were simple people. Our entertainment was an occasional movie or high school basketball game in Wheatland. We had company often (when the neighbors came over for a waffle supper), but we had no need of special flatware or china. We had no experience with formal entertaining. Now I felt inadequacy drowning me. *Do Cabinet wives' responsibilities include hostessing formal parties in our homes?* My throat was constricting from the panic I felt rising in my chest. *I don't like this,* I thought. *I'm not prepared.* It seemed that my background was not "right" economically, socially, or politically. *I don't want to be a liability to James.*

President Reagan's voice brought me back to the present. "We hear of special-interest groups. Well, our concern must be for a special-interest group that has been too long neglected. It knows no sectional boundaries, or ethnic and racial divisions, and it crosses political party lines. It is made up of men and women who raise our food, patrol our streets, man our mines and factories, teach our children, keep our homes, and heal us when we're sick. Professionals, industrialists, shopkeepers, clerks, cabbies, and truck drivers. They are, in short, 'We the people'—this breed called Americans."

I was stunned. *Why was my attention caught just then?* While I was struggling with fears of inadequacy, the President was mentioning the men and women who raise our food. *Farmers!* I was embarrassed by my relief, because my thoughts had been so immature. *That's the perspective I need. I represent a group of people and an area of our nation that needs recognition. Perhaps there are no other Cabinet wives from such a rural setting. Tonight, at the inaugural ball, when people ask me who I am, and where I come from, I will proudly say, "I'm a farmer's daughter from Wyoming!"* My heart went out to my parents. There were, of course, no cameras on me, but mentally I waved and mouthed, "Hello, Mom. Thanks, Dad," with a catch in my throat.

The President was now speaking of the monuments to Washington, Jefferson, and Lincoln that stood out in front of us that day. And beyond them, just across the Potomac River, was Arlington National Cemetery. He told of one young man whose body lies under one of those markers, Martin Treptow. He was killed in France while trying to carry a message between battalions under heavy artillery fire.

"We are told that on his body was found a diary. On the flyleaf under the heading 'My Pledge' he had written these words: 'America must win this war. Therefore I will work, I will save, I will sacrifice, I will endure, I will fight cheerfully and do my utmost, as if the issue of the whole struggle depended on me alone.' "

The President concluded his speech with this stirring challenge. "The crisis we are facing today does not require of us the kind of sacrifice that Martin Treptow and so many thousands of others were called upon to make. It does require, however, our best effort, and our willingness to believe in ourselves and to believe in our capacity to perform great deeds; to believe that together with God's help we can and will resolve the problems which now confront us. And, after all, why wouldn't we believe that? We are Americans."

Together we rose to applaud the challenge. The thunderous ovation extended on as if we were all joining in Martin Treptow's pledge. Then the Marine Band played the National Anthem, and it was like a call to action. We stood erect, never more proud to be Americans. As the final triumphant strains of the music faded, many on the platform cheered and hugged and clapped each other on the back.

The platform guests followed President and Mrs. Reagan back into the Capitol. I thought again of the President's words: ". . . together with God's help . . . ." It was not by chance that I had married James Watt. He had an important role to fill in this new Administration. But surely, so did I. Whatever my role was, I dedicated myself to do my best. The door that had opened before us scarcely one month earlier in Denver was the beginning of a new chapter of our lives.

CHAPTER THREE

THE PRESIDENT CALLS

The aroma of sugar cookies filled our house. I took another tray out of the oven and set the Christmas-shaped cookies on a cooling rack on the dining room table. I could see the twinkle of lights on the seven-foot Christmas tree that filled one side of our living room, its boughs covered with white paper angels, red ribbons, and white stars.

The sounds of Christmas music had me singing my favorite carols. In part, they were songs of gratefulness for the physical strength I felt after seven years of illness. I couldn't help but think of those awful times when I didn't have enough energy to do the simplest tasks, and when it hurt even to wear the lightest clothing. Doctors still hadn't diagnosed the problem, but some nutritional therapy had relieved the worst symptoms. Now that I could move around again, I no longer took the simple pleasures of life for granted.

This would be a special Christmas in Denver. We had moved here three years earlier from Maryland. Now our children were away at college. Our daughter, Erin, was planning to be married in a few months, and Eric had made a commitment to prepare for the ministry. Though I would miss them, there was a feeling of joy in seeing them full-grown and ready to assume their places in the world. I looked forward to the opportunity to become more involved in my husband's work.

The phone interrupted my thoughts. I answered it on the second ring. It was Joe Coors, the man who had hired James as president of Mountain States Legal Foundation. "May I please speak to Jim?" he asked.

"I'm sorry, Joe, he's in Spokane. Is there something I can do to help you?"

"No. But is there a way I can reach him today?"

I gave him a phone number. Several hours later James called me.

"Are you sitting down?" he asked.

"Why?"

"I'm coming home first thing tomorrow."

"Why? What's happening?" James wasn't scheduled to return for another day.

"Well, Joe was calling at Senator Paul Laxalt's request. The Senator wanted to know if I would accept the job of Secretary of the Interior if the President offered it to me."

I sat down hard. "What did you tell him?"

"I told him that I would have no choice. You don't turn down the President!" We laughed together nervously, and I wanted to hug him through the phone.

"What happens next?"

"Sunday I have to fly to Washington to be ready to meet with the Senator."

"Can I tell the kids?" I asked as the timer rang. Between juggling cookie trays in and out of the oven, I heard James answer, "No, we can't tell anyone yet."

With this one phone call I knew my life would never

quite be the same again. As I hung up, all my controlled joy became a burst of praise. I thought about the phone call James had received four weeks earlier, immediately after Ronald Reagan's election. A member of the President's transition team wanted to know if his name could be put on the list of men being considered for various Cabinet and subcabinet positions. James had said no, which was a surprising response for him. It wasn't that he didn't feel qualified to perform any of the jobs. During his 15 years in Washington he had proved to be a capable administrator, able to handle a wide range of responsibilities. But he also realized that he was a good salesman, and if he were being considered for a high-level office, he might be able to manipulate himself into position to win that job. That's how many people played this political game. James was willing to go back to Washington, but not eager. If he were going to go, he was determined that it be by invitation, not by anything he might do to get the job.

I turned to the refrigerator for the next batch of cookie dough and saw on the door a tattered news story. A couple of weeks after the election we had received this clipping out of the *New York Times* from an old friend, Doug Baldwin, who was directing the office of communications for the Interstate Commerce Commission. The story quoted the outgoing Secretary of the Interior, Cecil Andrus, as saying that the new Reagan Administration "will be able to make few, if any, major changes in the next four years in the slow, cumbersome way the nation's natural resources are developed and regulated." My husband felt that was probably a fair assessment. He suggested that we fulfill our Christian commitment to pray for our leaders. So I fastened the clipping to our refrigerator in order to remind us to pray for the man who would face this frustrating job.

The Secretary of the Interior is responsible for administering more than 750 million acres of federal land, most of it west of the Mississippi River, which is why the post was usually filled by a Westerner. He supervises a department of 80,000 employees who have far-ranging responsibilities including management of national parks, mineral development, water resources, and Indian reservations. James knew the inner workings of the Department, having served as Senator Simpson's aide on the Senate Interior Committee and later having served 3½ years as a developer and then 3½ years as a preservationist within the Department. He was aware that pressures were being exerted by environmental lobbyists and that, with the election of Jimmy Carter in 1976, hundreds of environmental activists received appointments in the Department. Under their direction, activities in areas such as federal coal leasing, oil and gas development, federal minerals land leasing, and water development had come to a virtual halt. Maintenance and protection of our National Park System had been neglected.

Reagan's first choice for this difficult post was Clifford Hansen, former U.S. Senator from Wyoming and a good friend of ours. Senator Hansen deliberated for two weeks before deciding that his long-term grazing leases with the Bureau of Land Management, an agency he would control, would provide an insurmountable conflict of interest. He finally told the President that he would have to decline the nomination.

On Sunday, December 7, James flew to Washington, D.C., to meet with Senator Laxalt. We could not breathe a word of this possibility to anyone. I was an excited woman, dying to tell my friends the good news, yet forced to keep the secret.

James met with Senator Laxalt on Monday for two grueling hours. Playing the role of devil's advocate, James suggested potential objections that might arise in the Senate confirmation hearings. That night he told me on the phone, "I made it plain that I'm not going to sell myself to the Reagan Administration. They are going to have to buy me as I am." James concluded from the Senator's enthusiasm that he was likely to be recommended to the President-elect.

"What kind of questions did Senator Laxalt ask?" I wondered.

"He wanted to know how I would rule on specific issues pending at Interior. So one-by-one we went through the issues. I gave him my gut answers, and he seemed to like my stance."

"Was he concerned whether or not you could handle the job?" I didn't understand how Cabinet officers were selected.

"Yes, but not from a substantive point of view. He wanted to know if I was tough enough. Could I take the pressure from a hostile press? Could I withstand the attacks on my personal life and family members? Could we take the abuse of the environmentalists?"

"Can you? Can we?" My heart began to beat faster.

James laughed and said, "I told the Senator, 'No man knows how tough he is until he has been in the fire. I'll tell you after I have done the job.' "

Tuesday, James had to lie low. On Wednesday afternoon he met with Reagan's key political advisers—Edwin Meese, James Baker, and Fred Fielding. They invited him to meet with Ronald Reagan the next day. Now it was time to tell the children and our parents. We all were numbed by this unimaginable opportunity.

Thursday I picked up the *Denver Post* from the front doorstep and opened it to find the headline: "Denverite Heads List For Top Interior Post." The article included an extensive biography of James and a quote by Joe Coors saying that James was "tremendously capable and qualified for the job." James had told me that the story would be deliberately leaked by Washington to test political reaction.

The newspaper account heightened my excitement. Friends and neighbors called, but the hours crawled by as I waited for James to call me that evening. The thought of James as a Cabinet officer, and of meeting the President, and of all the elaborate social functions was unbelievable. We were both 42 years old, but I felt as though we were just kids from Wyoming. Now my husband's name would be in history books. I thought of the days in Wheatland when I'd had to memorize the Cabinet positions for social studies class. I'd promptly forgotten them after the test.

The call finally came late in the evening. James sounded tired but excited. I wanted to know all about his meeting the President-elect.

"It was at the Blair House, across the street from the White House. President Reagan was very cordial. He invited me to accept the nomination as Secretary of the Interior, and I accepted."

"But how did it happen? Give me some details!" I laughed.

"We agreed on five major objectives for the Department. First, we want to reopen public lands to multiple use and to reduce our national dependence on foreign energy sources. Second, improve the quality and management of our national wildlife refuges. Third, establish a strategic minerals policy. Fourth, restore the national parks, which have been allowed to seriously deteriorate. And fifth, provide strong leadership for the Department, including our American Indians. The whole meeting lasted just 20 minutes."

"Boy, am I impressed by the way you ticked off those objectives. What else did you talk about?"

"I told the President that I was committed to this program and would make it work for America, whatever the price I personally had to pay. I explained that to bring the dramatic change we had outlined would be very controversial and that the press and paid environmentalists would create tremendous controversy. I told him I probably would not be able to survive politically more than 18 months if I stuck with our agenda to restore America. I told him, 'You're going to have to back me and back me and back me. When you can no longer back me, you will have to fire me.' "

A sudden stab of fear clutched my heart. *Why did he mention that? Certainly he can do the job, so what is the concern?* "What did the President say to that?"

"His eyes sparkled when he said, 'I will.' " As we hung up, I laughed at my anxious thoughts. Few people even knew the name of the Secretary of the Interior, much less what he did. Certainly there was nothing to fear.

James flew back to Denver the next day, and at the request of the President-elect we had to maintain a low profile for ten days until he made the announcement official. Members of the press camped on our front lawn. In order for James to get to work and wrap up loose ends at the Foundation, he had to climb the fence behind our house, where his vice-president, Steve Shipley, would pick him up. We received hundreds of phone calls from well-wishers, long-lost friends, and job seekers. The kids, who had come home for Christmas break, helped me answer all those calls. Whenever James was home we would repeat the caller's full name so James could hear and indicate whether he wanted to take the call personally. If a member of the press called, we simply said, "He's not giving any statements right now." It was fun, and I loved the involvement. Our whole family was caught up in the excitement.

James returned to Washington for the official announcement, after which he met with the press for the first time. I watched him that evening on the local news.

"What do you intend to do as Secretary?" they asked. James answered, "Serve the President." They tried to pin him down on several specific issues. But outside of a few general statements reaffirming the President's campaign platform, he made no commitments. Rather than forecast his plans for the future, he was following a long-standing personal conviction: Do something first, then talk about it later.

Christmas was a joyous celebration. Family discussion progressed naturally from Jesus as God's new beginning to everyone's new assignment for the coming year. That night James and I lay in bed and talked about our future. "You know what the little girl next door asked me yesterday?" I said to him. "She wanted to know if she could tell her eighth-grade class that she had watched Mr. Watt empty the garbage!"

James laughed and asked, "What did you tell her?"

"I said sure and added that she could also tell them that she'd seen you mow the lawn and wash the car and do all the things good dads do."

"You know, Lani, that's right," he said soberly. "We're just regular people, and I hope and pray that this job doesn't change that. All of us in the Administration are ordinary people. It helps to remember that the other men have probably all taken out the garbage."

"You know, it's so obvious to me that God has opened this door for you." I recounted some of the things that had impressed me. "I haven't told you this, but that night when you read in the paper that Senator Hansen had declined the nomination, I was reading the story over your shoulder. I had the strongest impression that you were going to get the nomination."

Senator Paul Laxalt of Nevada, a major principal in Reagan's victory, had been the man responsible for choosing the President's Secretary of the Interior. After Hansen had declined the position, Laxalt invited four

fellow senators to advise him on other potential candidates. One of them was a good friend, Senator Alan
Simpson of Wyoming. Senator McClure of Idaho, a man
James didn't know very well, suggested, "What about
Jim Watt?" Senator Simpson responded, "Well, I'll
be . . . I'm stunned at the brilliance of the idea." The other
two senators had agreed—being well acquainted with
his work—but Laxalt didn't know James. Senator Simpson gave him more details: "Jim Watt is the man who
can grab that monster by the throat and make it behave.
He knows where all the bones are buried. He knows
where the deadwood accumulates. He knows where all
the conduits and shunts and leaks are. He knows the
bureaucracy." Laxalt wanted to know, "Will he take the
job if asked?" And so the call had come from Joe Coors
in early December.

We cuddled together for a few minutes. Then I whispered, "Honey, I'm very proud of you. I'm looking forward to being with you in this challenge."

James chuckled, "You know, my 'old wife' wouldn't
have said that!"

As James drifted off to sleep, I reveled in his compli-
ment. So many changes had taken place in my life in
the years since we had moved to Denver. He was right.
Only in the last two years had I learned what it meant
to be truly involved in my husband's life, and had found
the emotional strength to do it. For many years I was
unable to give him the companionship he needed. Now
I thanked God for the changes He had made in me,
and for the opportunity to return to Washington. *And
Lord, while I'm praying, please give me the extra
strength I'll need during these next few weeks.*

After Christmas the excitement of the nomination
quickly faded as we faced the reality of the difficult job
James had to do. Even before the official announcement, sniping from environmental leaders began. A

representative of the National Audubon Society commented, "I'm very concerned. I hope it doesn't mean a giveaway of the nation's resources." A spokesman for the Wilderness Society called the appointment "disastrous." Another spokesman for that group said James represented "a naive and simplistic philosophy."

It was hard to understand these attacks. Twelve of the larger environmental groups sent a telegram to Reagan urging him to find another nominee "who can better try to represent the public interests in managing and conserving the nation's economic, cultural and natural resources." Reagan defended James by saying, "Jim Watt has only opposed environmental extremists. I think he's an environmentalist himself, as I am."

At the formal press conference following the nomination, James had read a prepared statement. "The tremendous complexities and statutory requirements vested in the Secretary's office fill that job with conflict and controversy. . . . Acting under the law, he must choose actions that will insure common sense, balanced perspectives in managing lands and waters subject to the multiple-use concepts which have been hammered out by Congress." James reviewed his record, which he felt demonstrated his commitment "to the fundamental values of America" and a balanced perspective between reasonable development of energy resources and preservation of our natural environment.

The next day the *New York Times* quoted William Turnage of the Wilderness Society as saying James Watt was "a joke" and "a caricature of an anticonservationist. You have to go back to Teapot Dome to find a Secretary of the Interior so totally out of step with society."

"James, look at this. What are they saying? Tell me about Teapot Dome again." I had to admit I didn't remember the details.

"Oh, you remember. That involved the scandal with

Sinclair Oil and Albert Fall, the Secretary of the Interior in the early 1920s." I remembered now that Fall was indicted for conspiracy and accepting bribes after he leased Teapot Dome fields to Sinclair Oil without competitive bidding.

"But why would they compare you to *that* scandal?"

"They are the same partisan voices that opposed Ronald Reagan's election. They don't seem interested in facts, or in giving me or the President a chance."

I couldn't help but wonder, *Why did they use such harsh, ugly words in commenting on James? Why don't they try to help? Is everything just political in Washington? Don't they want the President to be successful?* I really didn't understand the whys of the attack. James had done nothing wrong. He wasn't even in office.

Perry Pendley, who became one of James' first appointments, flew out to Denver to begin briefing him for the Senate hearing, which was scheduled for January 7. These days were going to be crucial for the confirmation. In 1968 James had been selected for President Nixon's transition team to help prepare Alaska's Governor Walter Hickel, the nominee for Interior Secretary, for his confirmation hearings. James had learned a lot from that experience. The environmental lobbyists were beginning to assert themselves in those days, and they put intense pressure on Hickel during the hearings. Trying to gain favor with the movement, Hickel made crucial concessions that seriously hindered his effectiveness once he was confirmed. Nixon finally fired him after less than two years in office. James never forgot the experience and was determined not to make the same mistakes.

There was only one brief interruption of his cram course—a breakfast meeting with representatives of several environmental groups on December 30. James invited them to tell or ask him anything they wanted, promising to be absolutely candid in his responses. The meeting lasted two hours. On some of the issues he had to admit he was not well-informed, but he listened to their views. Afterward he felt good about the session, and was hopeful that a bridge could be built between them. The leaders, while not supportive of James when talking to the press, did not denounce him, calling the time "a get-acquainted session to exchange views."

James flew to Washington for good on January 1, 1981, and left me with the job of selling our house and organizing the move. We had talked about renting or buying a small townhouse or condominium in Washington—something that would be easy to maintain with his workload and my health. It was hard for me to accept the fact that we would not be in a home with an open yard, but James needed to be close to work, and he was taking a cut in salary to serve the President. We simply couldn't afford a house.

After James set the selling price for our house, the rest was up to me. A businessman who was moving into Denver offered to buy the house at a price 2000 dollars less than we were asking. I knew little about how homes were bought and sold. But since James rarely compromised once he had made a decision, I figured the price was not negotiable. "My husband would never lower the price of his house," was my firm answer. "We would be glad to sell to you at our price."

The man accepted. Then I told him, "There's one other thing that needs to be in our contract."

"What's that?" he asked.

"The sale has to be contingent on my husband being confirmed by the Senate as Secretary of the Interior."

"Okay, let's write up the contract."

That quickly our house was sold! The next step was to choose the furniture we would take to Washington. There was far too much of it for a small townhouse, yet there wasn't time to sell it. So I gave it away to some Cambodian refugees who were being resettled by a church in Denver. I also gave them extra towels and linens. Our piano went to our church youth group. Tapes and books were given to the church library. Our encyclopedias and other books were donated to a new Christian school. There was no way our 1972 Ford Pinto could make it 2000 miles to the East Coast, so I gave it to a woman in the church. As I gave all those material possessions away, I was exhilarated.

I made arrangements for movers to come, and I packed 72 boxes by myself, amazed that I possessed such strength. A couple of times each day I would tire, but a ten-minute nap was enough to rejuvenate me.

The night before I was scheduled to fly to Washington to join James for the inauguration, I lay exhausted in bed, surrounded on all sides by open boxes. Despite the physical exhaustion, my spirit was full of joy. No matter how hard I tried, I couldn't sleep.

I remembered that James had made the bold statement in a press conference, "I am prepared intellectually, emotionally, and spiritually for this job." Friends had cautioned him not to mention "spiritual." "Why not?" was his rhetorical reply. "It's true."

It had been in relinquishing the life of our critically ill daughter that James had gained the resolve to follow God regardless of difficult circumstances. I could sense by his prayers at dinner that he considered this strength of purpose invaluable for the Cabinet post. He was ready. But was I?

How does it feel to be in his boat? I laughed at my own question, thinking back to the day five years earlier when my attitude toward James started changing. It was in Maryland, while I was suffering from an undiagnosed muscle disease, that God began inviting me to become the woman He envisioned. That morning I had attended a Bible study, and the exertion had left me exhausted. As I rested on the couch, my thoughts dwelt on the topic of our study. We were examining submission, particularly as it related to wives and husbands.

I held the erroneous view that submission meant doing what James wanted me to do—giving in. When he made a decision, I followed it whether I agreed with it or not. My silence, however, was not submission. It was a symptom of disrespect I had for myself and for him. It was a mask that allowed me to avoid my pent-up feelings and the mental accusation, "Christians don't act that way, you know." Our relationship was not fulfilling because we had lost our language of sharing.

I was miserably aware that James was frustrated with our relationship. For two years I had been unable to give him any of the comfort or pleasure that one might reasonably expect from his wife, for I had been almost an invalid. He had tried valiantly to be tender and understanding of my condition, often even carrying me up and down the stairs when I was too weak to make it on my own. But I was not a companion. I didn't even know what he was doing in his work. And I really didn't care. The medication that had given me temporary relief had also left me puffy and bloated. I looked mannish and felt ugly. For weeks on end, life seemed to go on without me.

As I lay on the couch that particular morning, I saw the picture in my mind—two rowboats, each with a seat and a set of oars. Somehow I knew they represented James and me. We were connected by a thick rope that gave me a very secure feeling. I was still attached to my husband, yet free to stay behind if I wanted, or to speed up ahead of him, or to come alongside and poke him with an oar.

As I "viewed" the cartoon, I saw words above it, like a neon sign: "Get into his boat." Panic filled me. For the first time I realized I had totally missed the meaning of submission. I was only acquiescing to my husband to avoid turmoil in the family. But our lives were not integrated. I didn't know what he was thinking. I didn't know where he was hurting, or what gave him happiness. I had little desire or strength to try to share in his life. As long as he provided for the children and me, I didn't worry about what my husband was doing at work. I was very comfortable in my own boat, doing whatever I wanted for myself and, I thought, for God.

It scared me to think of the implications of getting into James' boat. There was only one set of oars, and James would be rowing. What if he went too fast? What if we capsized? I hated water. I didn't want him taking any chances, and I knew he dared to take risks. But God was speaking to me. He wasn't giving me an option. His command was clear: "Get into his boat." "Lord," I prayed, "I don't know how to do this. Make me willing to follow Your command. Make me the wife that James Watt needs."

I knew the first thing I needed to do was to tell my husband. It was several days before I had the courage. "James, can we talk a minute?" I asked, sitting in our car after church. I began to tell him about the cartoon in my mind and God's instructions. "I realize I have not been the wife I should be," I said, then stopped to choke back the tears. "I have not even been in your boat. I haven't been traveling your direction." I was quiet for a moment. James said nothing, staring past me with his head tilted back against the window. "James, I want to get in your boat," I said meekly.

It was a terrifying moment. For the first time I found myself completely vulnerable. No longer would I be in control of my life. Though I had been married to this man for 15 years, I had only displayed the appearance of unity. Now I had to really practice it. A tired smile came across James' face as he finally looked over at me. "Glub, glub, glub!" was all he said.

From my husband, I should have expected a quip. He has a gift for using humor to relieve tense situations. But this time I didn't appreciate it. I opened the door, got out, and, with all the strength I could muster in my sick body, slammed it shut. I didn't even try to hold back the tears as I walked into the house. It had cost me so much to be willing to try to get out of my boat and into his, and there was no turning back. The least he could have done was show some appreciation. He had acted as though he had no comprehension of what I had really shared with him. I had wondered how I could trust him with my life if I wasn't sure he cared. The thought of going down with his ship wasn't funny.

I could remember, a few months later, in 1975, attending a ceremony where James was sworn in as a member of the Federal Power Commission. I had expected our family and maybe a couple of close friends to attend. Instead, more than 250 people had packed the walnut-paneled Senate meeting room and overflowed into the hall. Until then I had no idea that my husband was so respected by his associates.

The months prior to that ceremony had been embarrassing for James. President Ford made the appointment, but an anonymous accusation against James delayed Senate confirmation for six months. James was finally cleared of any wrongdoing, but I had been practically oblivious to the problem. Remembering that experience helped me understand why God had told me to get into my husband's boat. If we had been going the same direction with similar goals, submission would have ceased to be an effort or an issue.

Knowing the answer did not make the last five years easy. There were more medical failures as well as new hopes for me, the uprooting of our high-school-age children for the move here to Denver, and the serious illness of our daughter. Tonight was my last night in our Denver home. Tomorrow the movers would come. Weariness was finally capturing my excited mind, and for a sleepy moment I longed to be next to James. Here in Denver God had showed me how to get into his boat. Finally, after years of resistance, God had made me the wife that James Watt needed. And not a moment too soon.

CHAPTER FOUR

WIFE IN THE PRESSURE COOKER

The reception desk was vacant as I entered the Commercial Settlement office. A row of people were seated on a beige-print sofa and several wooden chairs, as if waiting their turn to see a dentist. This was where I was supposed to complete the closing on our new home—a townhouse in northwest Washington.

Too nervous to ask any questions, I sat in the only open chair and silently said another prayer. Whatever glamour I might have felt during and after the inauguration had now dissipated. My husband was immersed in his work from dawn until late at night. Three or four evenings each week, we were expected to appear at one or more social functions. James was usually exhausted when he arrived home and would fall into bed, only to rise the next morning and repeat the process.

Up till now James had always handled our finances. But now I was left to manage our budget. James had done a preliminary search for a home when he flew to Washington to meet with Senator Laxalt. He wanted a small condominium or townhouse, something easy to maintain and close to work. Our entertaining, we discovered, would be done outside the home.

James had found what he wanted and described it to me when I came to Washington. I contacted a friend who was a real estate agent and located a place that fit James' description—a small, cheerful home with large windows. Later I learned that it was in a different development from the one he described. I was thankful that James liked it. Until we closed escrow on the townhouse, we were staying with friends.

James had promised several times in recent days to find a lawyer to represent us at the closing, but in the press of his work he had forgotten. This morning he suddenly realized he was sending his wife, who was still not completely well and who had no business experience, off to the closing without any help. We knew several lawyers in Maryland, but none who could practice in the District of Columbia.

James felt terrible, but he was unable to drop his appointments. I called a friend and asked if he knew a lawyer who could meet me at the settlement office. He said he would see what he could do, but he would be unable to report back to me before I left the house. So either someone showed up or I was on my own.

In order to be of some help, James provided his chauffeured car to take me to the meeting. On the way over I prayed fervently, though I was amazed at my calmness. *Lord, You've brought me this far. You've helped me sell our house in Denver, and hire the movers, and find this home. Surely You will help me now at the closing. Lord, don't let there be any hitch. . . . Lord, please have a lawyer there.*

I continued to pray as I waited in the office. Finally one of the women seated with me asked, "Are you Mrs. Watt?" I said I was. "We've been waiting for you." It turned out everyone was there for my closing. There was the developer, his real estate agent, the banker handling the mortgage money, and a representative of the settlement office. The last man to introduce himself said, "I'm your lawyer." I wanted to shout, "You're an answer to prayer!"

We were escorted to a conference table, and the six of us sat and reviewed the papers. I explained that our house had sold in Denver, but the money hadn't cleared escrow. It would be available within the week. They accepted that and we went through the contract. Of course, both my husband and I needed to sign the papers. "I'll sign these now in your presence and take them to my husband's office. He'll sign them there."

"Well, that's rather unusual procedure," said the agent.

"It's going to have to be that way," I said apologetically. "He doesn't have time to come down here."

"Don't you think," asked the lawyer with a laugh, "that we can trust someone the President has chosen?"

After the meeting I took the papers down to the Department of the Interior. Ralph Chinn, James' chauffeur, drove into the garage underneath the building and personally escorted me up the Secretary's private elevator. The first person I met as I exited onto the sixth floor was Kittie. Ralph introduced us, and Kittie led me past a group of men waiting to see James.

In his office, more men were sitting at the round table, where James was talking on the phone. "May I interrupt you?" I asked. "You've got these papers to sign."

He covered the phone with his hand, raised his eyebrows, and said, "Did you get 'em, Babe? Good for you!" As he continued his phone conversation, I pointed to the places for his signature and flipped all 15 pages while he signed them.

That afternoon, as soon as the furniture was unloaded, I plunged into the job of making our home a refuge, a place where James could escape from the pressures of his job. The warmth came from deep tones of wallpaper, antique oak furniture, and numerous plants, including two tall ficus trees.

I was proud of all I had accomplished in finding, purchasing, and setting up this home. I had never handled so much responsibility for our well-being, and I was elated to see that I could do it. I felt that if something were to happen to James, I could now cope. But that exhilaration soon wore off.

A few mornings later, after James had gone off to work, accusing thoughts began to nag my mind. *It isn't right that James has saddled me with all this responsibility. I can, of course, pay all the bills, but what about the other decisions concerning our home? If the furnace breaks down, will I have to see that it is fixed? Who's going to be responsible to see that the bricks are relaid to get rid of the puddle at our front door? Who's going to decide how the patio is finished? For all I know, I'll probably have to carry out the trash!*

I was shocked. *What am I doing railing like this?* Hadn't God provided whatever He required of me? Physical strength. Courage to ask for help. A calming presence in tense moments. Even a lawyer! And hadn't I relished James' recognition for my being capable? Hadn't I delighted in his respect for my initiative? I had even taken comfort in the fact that I felt I could cope if something happened to James. So what was my problem? Where did this anger come from?

When the tasks had seemed temporary, I had met the challenge with enthusiasm. But now, when it was clear that James would not be resuming his household responsibilities, and that others were going to be added, I resented it.

Lord, I don't like this, I complained. *I had to take care of our move from Denver, and sell the house and buy this home, and figure out the finances. I had to make all the decisions. Why did my husband ask me to do all this?*

In the middle of this tirade, the words cut across my mind: *Your husband did not ask you to do those things. . .I did.* I felt flattened. It had been many years since God had told me to get into my husband's boat. Now it was a reality. But staying in his boat was going to be tested.

Because of my morning grumbling, I was late for the weekly Cabinet wives' Bible study. I voiced a quick, *Forgive me, Lord, for my outburst. Thank You for reminding me that You direct my life.* I slipped into my winter coat, and on the way to the car chided myself for wasting time with angry thoughts.

I looked forward to the study and being with Susan Baker (senior White House staff wives were also invited), Sue Block, and Claire Schweiker. Ann Edwards and I walked together up the curved red stairway of Fellowship House and into the library. Barbara Priddy, a co-teacher, was pouring coffee or hot water for each of us as we arrived. Betty Ruth Bell and Betty James were already seated.

During our sharing time the subject turned to the increasing responsibilities we all faced. I admitted my negative thoughts of this morning, and that God had reminded me that it was not James who had given me the added responsibility. A discussion about coping with our feelings followed, and that reminded me of a graphic mental illustration—my pots-and-pans story—which I shared with the women.

"It happened two years ago. The best way to describe it is that it was an animated black-and-white drawing. There was a large stove with huge burners and several large pots on them—the size one would use to cook chili for 50 people. The lids were dancing on top of the pots, and puffs of steam were rising to the ceiling. It seemed that the purpose of my life was to keep the lids on those pots.

"After frantically trying to hold down the lids, I reached down to turn off the heat. Any cook knows that, within a minute, the lids on those pots will settle. As I stood back and began to relax, I saw a giant hand—and somehow I knew it was God's hand—reach down and turn the heat up as high as it would go. Soon the lids were dancing with a loud rattling noise and threatening to fly completely off the pots.

"I doubled my efforts to keep the lids on. Then cutting across my frantic actions, I heard these words, 'Leilani, if you would let Me cleanse those pots, you wouldn't have to worry about keeping the lids on.'

"Incredulous, I asked, 'What's in the pots?'

"The only word I heard was 'anger.' I quickly dismissed the whole thing because it certainly didn't describe me. If ever there was a person who was not angry, it was I. I was the most patient mother you'd ever seen. I never yelled at my children. I volunteered to teach kindergarten. I was never ruffled by hordes of giggly children. My husband knew me as a quiet, unassuming person, willing to defer to his better judgment. I always had a smile for the neighbor, even when his dog had kept me awake half the night. I meekly accepted the surly abuse of an irritable store clerk. I was simply not an angry woman. It was a ridiculous idea.

"But I couldn't erase that picture from my mind. A few days later I received a book called *What Wives Wish Their Husbands Knew About Women,* by Dr. James Dobson. After reading just a couple of pages, I grabbed a pencil and started making notes in the margins. My years of pent-up anger came out the end of that pencil and were starkly apparent in the heavy-handed writing on almost every page. I was angry at God for not healing me of my painful muscle disease. I was angry at my husband for pushing the children. I was angry at my brother for the vicious fights we had had as kids. There was no choice but to admit that I was an angry woman."

The other women could relate. Some told about their experiences before Sallie Clingman, our other leader, took us to the Bible for answers. We read I John 1:9, which seemed uncanny in its confirmation of the illustration I had just shared. To me it meant if I would own up to my guiltiness, God would always forgive my guilt and even scour away the deep-seated causes.

As I drove home after the study, I realized that I had not really dealt with my problem this morning. I had asked forgiveness for my grumbling. But I needed to apply the lessons of the pots and pans if I didn't want to have to keep pushing down the lids.

Back in the quiet of our home I addressed the half-finished issue. I had learned that asking forgiveness was a valuable and necessary step for starting over between any two people, or between me and God. However, I also recognized that I could easily repeat the same offense. I needed more than forgiveness to solve that problem. I needed to apply an answer I had learned two years before at a Bible study in Denver.

At first I had been attracted by the German accent of the speaker. She was from Phoenix and one of the Evangelical Sisters of Mary, a Lutheran sisterhood founded in Germany after World War II by Mother Basilea Schlink. Even more compelling than her accent was the story she shared of going a step beyond asking for forgiveness—to something she called repentance. She showed us from Scripture that God is a real Father who waits for His children to bring Him joy. I had never thought of my actions as affecting God in any way. Yet when I thought of how my own children's public behavior reflected on me as a parent, I could understand how my behavior was a reflection on my heavenly Father. If my actions affected God's feelings, I wanted to do more than obey Him; I wanted to please Him. If my wrong attitudes—the Sister called them sins— disappointed God, I wanted to change them.

The question was *how?* Asking for forgiveness dealt with *what* I did, and that was important. But the Sister explained how repentance could change the *why*. For me it was scouring the pots. I already knew that the reason my life could be changed at all was because of the life, death, and resurrection of Jesus Christ. But now I understood that if I faced my repeated failures, Jesus would show me two things: why I had failed and how that failure made God feel. It might be a painful discovery, because I would recognize that my refusal to accept God's help not only made me a poor example of Christianity, but also caused my Father grief. But then what would bring Him joy? When I could accept His remedy for my problem. Then He would give me peace and joy and cleanness through Jesus Christ. Experiencing the relief of honesty made me willing to take the lids off other areas of my life.

What about my angry diatribe this morning? *Lord, what is it that made me angry?* The answer came quickly and clearly: *Mistrust.* But I wondered, *What did coping with moving have to do with mistrust?* Even as I thought those words, the answer became clear. I had concluded that I would be able to handle my affairs even as a widow. But God wanted me to recognize that my real ability to cope came only from His continual provision. Providing a lawyer at the closing was a perfect example. The strength He gave me was another. I couldn't take credit for those things. Neither could I complain about added tasks. Fulfilling my new responsibilities was going to be possible only through God's provision.

That's it! Father, I see how my not trusting You was an insult. You are the Creator and Provider. Please forgive me. I was angry for receiving added responsibility because I knew I couldn't handle it alone. I want to give You all my mistrust. I want to turn toward You. Oh, thank You that You promise to supply all that I will need. You are a God who helps!

I laughed with relief. Repentance was a very important spiritual lesson I had learned. It allowed God to reveal the root cause of any problem. When I agreed with God and turned away from that sin toward Him, He was able to change me. I called Sallie to share my good news. She was excited and suggested that we have lunch together the next day.

We met at Quigley's, a turn-of-the-century cafe. We were seated in ice cream chairs at a table with a red-and-white cloth. "I appreciated your pots-and-pans story at Bible study," she said after the waiter took our orders. "Tell me how you got interested in spiritual things."

"Before I met James, I understood that God loved me and that He provided Jesus Christ to span the separation between us. When I was nine years old, I prayed to receive Jesus as my Savior. What I didn't understand was how to deal with my everyday anger and resentment. So I hid them. Over the years I wore a mask of composure. That meant I had to avoid any conflict which threatened to expose my weaknesses. Most of my friends never knew the turmoil that ruled inside me.

"After college James and I moved to Washington, and God began to help me. First He poured out His Holy Spirit upon me. The results were a sense of direction and a spiritual communication of prayer and praise. The Bible became interesting and understandable. Through Bible study I began to see myself as God saw me: acceptable, gifted, guided—and definitely in need of training and pruning. Nearly eight years ago, while I struggled with an undiagnosed muscle disease, God invited me to learn how to become the woman He wanted me to be."

"Tell me about your muscle disease, Leilani."

"Well, it's complicated by many factors. Although I've had a variety of doctors, there was never a single diagnosis they could agree on. Was it an immune or an enzyme problem? Was it mercury toxicity or biochemical imbalance? We've tried all of those avenues.

"Furthermore, we've experienced some dramatic physical healings in our family, yet I was not quickly healed through prayer. Instead I've made slow but steady physical and spiritual progress. The last time some of our government friends saw me, a few years ago, I was sight-seeing from a wheelchair. Now I can run up stairs! My family knows how I suffered with poor recall and decision-making capacities. Now I have a sharpened brain.

"I'm presently under a doctor's care for nutrition therapy. This powder you see me taking in Nystatin, an antibiotic for yeast sensitivity. The difference this latest breakthrough has made is glorious! James is particularly delighted because I can be with him when he travels and keep up with his schedule here in Washington. This has all come as an answer to prayer."

Our food arrived, but Sallie continued to ask questions. "How are you adjusting to the pressures of being a Cabinet member's wife?"

"I couldn't have handled this two years ago. Repentance was the key for me to be able to face the pressure. As I became honest with God, I had a greater desire to be close to my husband. Before, I would have run. One of the hardest things for me was to side with James—I'm sure you know what a forceful personality he has. I couldn't stand to see him push anyone in a discussion, so I always took the other side.

"I'll give you an example. James initiated dinner

discussions with our children before they were teenagers. Because he's a lawyer, he would deliberately take a stand which opposed the children's view. It didn't matter what the topic was—peer pressure, politics, the authority of Scripture, abortion—he insisted that they have an opinion and that they be able to defend it. I couldn't stand some of the arguments."

"What did you do?"

"Don't laugh! Many times my overreaction caused the kids to ask *me* to leave the table so the discussion could continue. 'Go to the basement, Mom,' became the byword. I literally would go to the basement to avoid the conflicts."

"How did your kids feel about those discussions?"

"They loved them, even when there were tears. They hardly ever missed dinner. They knew their dad valued their opinions and that their point of view could be heard. The kids are grown now, but they both know what they believe and why. These discussions have even become a Watt family-gathering tradition."

"And how do you feel about those discussions now?"

"Now that I'm not hiding my problems from God, I'm more secure. It's easier to be loyal to James. Isn't that amazing? In fact, James has started calling me his new wife!"

"What was the turning point?"

"Well, I was praying one day about my struggle with self-worth. I didn't have the stamina for a career, yet I was starving for some measure of my value. After I had poured out my heart to God, I heard one word: *Give*."

Sallie looked at me, a little puzzled.

"Really. When God told me to give, I was floored. *I* was the one who was in need. 'Give!' I blurted. 'I have nothing to give.' My protest was answered by several things I knew James needed from me: praise, respect, attention. But how could I give any of these things to him when I was so empty myself? It was a dilemma."

"How did you resolve it?"

"I looked up the rest of the verse in Luke 6:38: 'Give, and it will be given to you . . . . For whatever measure you deal out to others, it will be dealt to you in return.' What an answer! It seemed impossibly reversed to me, but it came from a Father I was learning to trust.

"I hardly knew how to begin. I had forgotten the words to use. I started searching for reasons to praise James—perhaps for taking a difficult legal case that cost him some uneasy moments; for counseling Erin even though there were tears; for defending Eric. As I continued to praise him, I found myself beginning to respect his stability and wanting to sit closer to him, to listen to him, to touch him. I was trusting that in some way I would receive the emotional support I needed.

"In time James began to respond. He began thanking me for the little things I did for him and for the character qualities he appreciated in me. When I put James' needs first in my thoughts, he began to put my needs first in his. It was like falling in love again. I had learned about praising the Lord, but I hadn't realized that the same things that had brought me closer to God could also bring me closer to James."

As we left the restaurant Sallie said, "Leilani, you have a tremendous opportunity to serve God here in Washington. I would like to set up some speaking engagements for you."

"Thanks, Sallie. But I'm not sure that's what I should be doing."

Back home I wondered why I had said that. Sallie's offer was very appealing. I enjoyed speaking and teaching. But there were also a lot of other ways to use my time. Cabinet wives had busy schedules that included benefit luncheons, teas, and style shows. However, even

with all these activities, we wives were often lonely. One way to counteract that was through special projects.

One potential project was helping in the restoration of Ellis Island and the Statue of Liberty, which was being supervised by the Department of the Interior. I had always had an interest in the millions of immigrants who suffered so much to come to the United States. They had contributed many important qualities to our nation. I was particularly interested in helping develop curricula for elementary and junior high schools to celebrate the centennial of the Statue of Liberty in 1986.

Other areas of interest were the antiabortion campaign and the antidrug-abuse program, a primary concern of Mrs. Reagan. There was also my personal interest in the development of the Holocaust Living Memorial. These were all significant projects that would have lasting value.

But how did God want me to use my time? I remembered a dramatic moment at a convention in Seattle in the midseventies when I had heard several messages about a type of prayer called intercession. From what I could understand, I knew I did not want to be an intercessor. It was described as a lawyer presenting a case on behalf of a client. Intercession demanded a considerable commitment of time for preparation and prayer. I did not want to stay at home and pray. Now that I could be up and around, I wanted to be with people, assuming leadership responsibilities. Besides, I was afraid that there were few tangible results in intercession. I needed to *do* something that made me feel valuable.

Yet, during a quiet moment at that meeting, I had heard these words in my mind: *Your husband is going to be on the front lines. If you will not pray for him, who will?* At the time that didn't make sense. *I do pray for him,* I thought. *Besides, I can pray for him and still do all these other activities.*

Now that James was Secretary of the Interior, I saw his need. My husband *was* on the front lines. But for a moment I was afraid. James was consumed by his new job and had little time for me. If I didn't have projects or meaningful relationships, would I be "starved" again? Would I experience emotional isolation, as I had in the past?

There were so many interesting things that could be satisfying—opportunities to work closely with people, to meet diplomatic wives, to sponsor programs that would give me a sense of accomplishment. However, to intercede meant being alone, devoting a significant portion of each day to praying for James. Though I had learned the importance of intercession, there was no guarantee that the results could be measured. Sallie's invitation was tempting because at least I could talk to people about God. Intercession meant that my primary involvement in Washington would be talking to God about people.

I weighed all the possibilities, but I could not avoid the lessons I had learned in Denver. They also applied to my life in Washington. My decision was that I would give because that was God's way. My commitment to Him was to give to James, which included giving him my time in intercession. A bubbling joy accompanied my decision. On my bulletin board by the kitchen phone I read again, with renewed impact, these words from the Sisters of Mary: "Whatever we do out of love for God is rewarding, even if no one sees." Rewarding indeed! The remaining portion of Luke 6:38 read, "Give, and it will be given to you; good measure, pressed down, shaken together, running over, they will pour into your lap" (NASB). I was curious to see how that would happen.

As I set myself to intercede, I was not dismayed by the usual thoughts and circumstances that distracted me. However, after several days of difficulty I was disturbed about a subtle challenge to my commitment to remain at home. I became increasingly fearful of leaving the house or appearing in the Washington social setting. One morning I called our daughter in Tulsa and told her about my problem. "Mom, that's just a spirit of fear. You hang up the phone and let's both pray." I knew that when Erin prayed she meant business. I had only started down the hallway to the living room when I felt the whole presence of fear leave me. With relief I realized that the feelings of isolation were gone. My commitment to intercede had passed the first of many tests.

To practice intercession effectively, I set aside a definite time each day—making an actual appointment—in a comfortable place. In a corner of the living room opposite the patio door were an antique oak rocker and a little table. Together with a songbook, a Bible, and a notebook, these comprised my prayer corner. Prayer time began almost immediately after James left for work.

Usually I started with a daily devotional, reading Scripture and singing appropriate songs of worship. The variety was pleasant, and often the context of the Scripture inspired me to continue in a short Bible study. In previous years I had spent about 15 minutes nearly every day in this manner, with a similar amount of time allotted to prayer for family and other concerns.

However, intercession was work, and it often required most of the morning. I had a lot to learn about the preparation necessary to approach a loving and holy God. About listening to the heart of a Father before I made my request known. About the humility of praying on behalf of James, our nation, and persecuted Jews and Christians behind the Iron Curtain. About the perseverence required on days when I felt empty. About claiming promises available to me in Scripture. As the weeks passed, I finally began to exult in the challenge of being an intercessor and, in the process, of helping to bear my husband's burdens.

These times of prayer helped knit me to my husband spiritually and emotionally. Not only did he appreciate my prayer for him, but when he realized my commitment to God to pray for him, he did everything possible to protect that time. His approval was a bonus, for I would have had to continue this ministry of intercession even if he had never noticed.

Because of James' busy schedule, I found special ways to make the most of our times together. One was to sit together at dinner parties. According to Washington protocol, you don't sit with your husband. At best, you are across the table from him; often you're at separate tables. It is a marvelous way to meet new people and discover the interesting facets of their lives. But James and I needed time together, so we switched the place cards and I sat next to him. It was six months before we were soundly reprimanded for this practice and decided to stop. But by then we had found an even better way to spend extra time together.

I loved the excitement of the Department. I wanted to know enough about James' work to pray intelligently for him, and to listen with understanding to all the messages I received for him as we traveled. James invited me to come to the office during open staff time any evening that we also had an engagement after work.

It was a privilege to listen to his top management team come into the office without appointment and talk over their problems. The tone of the meeting was relaxed, yet intense. With everyone propping his feet on the round desk, James would hear reports about the day, receive calls from Western offices, and listen to options on important issues. When an issue reached James, it usually meant decision time. What a thrill it was to see James and his team debate an issue and reach their conclusions!

During these meetings I was able not only to begin to understand his problems, but to actually feel what he was feeling. By sharing his most intimate emotions, a deeper loyalty developed in me. One evening on the 5:30 news, I heard about a vicious charge against him and I knew James would be under pressure to resign. When I heard his key in the door, I ran for the bottom step on the stairwell so I would be tall enough to hug him. "What are you doing up there?" he asked when he came in.

"Come here!" I threw my arms around him and gave him a huge bear hug. "There's trouble again, Honey. Have you heard the news?"

"Yeah."

"Glub, glub, glub!" I whispered in his ear. We both laughed. He caught the important message in those words. I was irrevocably committed to being in his boat, and if he were going down, then I was going to go down with him!

With that commitment came tremendous peace. Gone were the pretense and fear of isolation with which I had struggled for years. I had discovered that true happiness did not come from deciding what *I* wanted to do. True fulfillment came from being the woman God intended me to be, and from trusting in His plan for my life. The highest priority of my life became serving God by being the wife that James Watt needed. We were two people who delighted in being together. We were the most intimate of friends, able to trust each other with our deepest thoughts. I was convinced that together, through God's strength, we could face any problem.

CHAPTER FIVE

DUMP WATT! DUMP WATT!

"**L**ani, listen to this!" We had just finished dinner and were relaxing in the living room. James liked to stretch out on the floor, his back resting against the couch. I was sitting next to him when he reached into his briefcase and pulled out some papers. "This is a questionnaire. I'm going to ask you a few of the questions and you tell me how you'd answer."

"Okay," I said, curious as to what this might be. James had a little gleam in his eye, so I was on guard for a joke.

"This survey was sent out to members of the National Wildlife Federation. There's a statement, then a question and two or three options to choose from. Okay?"

"Ready."

"First I'll read the issue. 'The National Park System is administered by the Department of the Interior. A wide variety of recreational activities are encouraged within national parks. Some activities such as mining and timber cutting are not allowed. There is a current backlog of nearly 500,000 acres already authorized for purchase by Congress, but not yet acquired.'

"Now here's the question. 'The Federal Government is currently thinking of changing some of its policies about the national parks. Please choose the one you most prefer. One: No new national park areas should be acquired by the Federal Government. Instead the money saved should be used to manage the existing parks better. Two: Although improvements should be made in managing existing national parks, we still need to spend money to acquire those new park areas which Congress has already approved. Three: It is hard to choose between the two positions. Four: I don't know.' "

I thought for a moment before answering. "Well, if Congress has already approved new park areas, it seems to me we should move to purchase them and also improve our present parks."

"Okay, here's the second question. 'The National Park Service professionals should continue to make decisions about what facilities (lodges, roads, parking lots, airboat rides, etc.) are best for the national parks and how they should be managed.' Or your other choice is that 'commercial companies operating facilities in the national parks should have greater say over how the parks are managed and what facilities should be provided."

"Well, that's easy," I answered. "The park service professionals should make those decisions."

"Final question. You have two choices. 'A, we should continue to add to the list of endangered species when the biological evidence warrants such listings; otherwise these species will not be adequately protected from extinction. Or B, no more species should be added to the list, even if evidence shows they are endangered, because adding more would create further conflict with commercial development.' "

"A. Definitely, A."

"Congratulations! You've just voted to fire James

Watt, and I've only been in office six months."

"What!" I reached over to put my arm around his shoulders and looked at the survey he was holding.

"Don't feel bad. When Doug asked me those questions at the office, I also fired James Watt."

"But I don't get it. If you agree with the environmentalists, then why do they want you fired?"

"The questions and answers are skewed. They've misstated the Department policies. Nothing I do or say will change their preconceived ideas. The membership of the National Wildlife Federation has been a very conservative group. Two-thirds of the members voted for President Reagan in the last election. Yet according to this survey, created by their paid staff, they overwhelmingly reject 10 out of 11 of what they *think* are my positions.

"The Sierra Club has announced that it's going to try to collect one million signatures demanding that I be fired as Secretary of the Interior. They opposed me six months ago at my Senate confirmation hearings and they have opposed me every day since without giving me a chance. They obviously are determined to play their political game regardless of what I do."

I moved up on the couch behind James and began to massage his shoulder muscles. "So what are you going to do?" I asked.

"It's time for me to start traveling in order to get the truth out. For six months the paid environmentalists in Washington have had their free say without concern for fact or truth. Now we have to go out and tell people what we've accomplished. I think they'll be pleasantly surprised when they hear the facts.

"Let me show you what I mean. The introduction to this questionnaire states: 'Every effort was made to accurately portray Secretary Watt's philosophy on these issues. Because he has not precisely defined his position on every one of the issues surveyed, there may be variances between his actual position and the position in the questionnaire which we consider to be his.'

"This is what we're fighting against. They're presenting as fact what they perceive to be my position rather than my actual stand. For example, the first question— my position is stated that we won't purchase any more park land. That's not true. We've simply shifted priorities from land acquisition until existing parks are protected and upgraded to current health-and-safety standards. In the past the Department has not been a good steward of the land we have, and until we are, we should be careful about purchasing more. I have always called for more purchase of park land. Hopefully, after the President's economic recovery, we can spend 400 to 600 million dollars a year acquiring park land.

"Now take the last question I asked you. Do you realize that the previous Administration added numerous endangered species while failing to develop adequate recovery plans, which is also mandated by Congress? So species can die out while on the list. We're redirecting our efforts to help species' *recovery* as well as listing those which are threatened."

When he stopped talking, I clapped and gave my husband a rousing cheer. "That was fantastic! What a speech. The people don't know that. Give them the facts!"

So James hit the road, and many times I traveled with him, especially when he spoke for the Republican party. These were exciting trips. Party members came to hear James in record numbers, and he was admired for his tough stand for the President. Key groups were targeted for his presentations, such as the Western governors, state legislators, and special-interest groups. Only a half-dozen or so of the environmental groups were making the most noise against James Watt. There were more than 200 groups who were directly affected by one or more areas under Interior Department jurisdiction—groups such as cattlemen, miners, sportsmen, bikers, and park concessioners. They weren't protesting. They were cheering. James appeared before as many of these groups as possible.

The Republican fund-raisers were the most fun. At one party we waited offstage as local party dignitaries were introduced individually to the crowd of more than 1000 people. There was warm applause as each introduction was made. Finally, James and I were the only ones not at their places at the head table. Then the announcer, with a dramatic flourish, said: "And now, ladies and gentlemen, our special guest tonight. He's served our great nation and the Republican party faithfully for the last 20 years—a man unafraid to tell it like it is. He's the Secretary of the Interior for our great President. Please give a warm welcome to James Watt!"

The final words were drowned out by the noise as the crowd began to cheer wildly. James hated these embellished introductions and wanted to walk quickly to his seat. But the crowd wouldn't allow it. We entered the bright lights, and I could see streamers being unfurled and banners and placards with phrases such as "We Love James Watt" and "I Know Watt's Right" being pumped enthusiastically. In the back of the banquet hall a huge red-white-and-blue banner announced, "Welcome James Watt." Responding to the show of affection, James waved to the crowd, then encouraged them to sit down. But the decibel level just increased. It was at least three minutes before they allowed us to take our seats. It warmed my heart to hear supporters for James, since the news focused mainly on the controversies.

The ovation was repeated when James was introduced as the speaker. I loved to hear him speak. There

Panning for gold in Fairbanks, Alaska

were many victories to report. In six months James had accomplished what many thought was impossible. He had brought the Department of the Interior under control. The nation's park facilities were being upgraded after four years of neglect. Several regulating functions were being turned over to the states, as Congress had mandated, easing excessive federal control of the mining industries. Mineral surveys on public lands, long ignored despite Congressional order, were being accelerated. Offshore oil and gas exploration were opening up under strict environmental guidelines. James reported these and many other accomplishments, often using an overhead chart that showed figures from the public record.

Despite such enthusiastic support, it was obvious that the environmentalists were winning through the press in their campaign to discredit James. Through the news media they kept a constant barrage of misinformation before the public. At this rate it seemed unlikely that he could remain in office for long. One presidential adviser was quoted as saying, "He's probably got a short political life." *Time* magazine stated, "Watt has been told to clear major policy announcements with the White House so that image-conscious aides can try to mute any potential public outcry." There was no truth whatever to the statement, but the public didn't know that.

By now my husband's portrait was familiar to most Americans. All three major news weeklies did major stories on him. And for their art, they often chose photographs or caricatures of him with an arrogant or snooty expression. It is a Watt family habit, when they are thinking or listening to someone, to tilt back their heads. Photographers learned to wait for that pose in order to portray James as a cocky, uncompromising demagogue. Cartoonists were having a field day, with literally hundreds of drawings of James with oil derricks growing out of his bald head, carrying a chain saw, driving a bulldozer, shooting Smokey the Bear, and bagging Santa's reindeer.

I was encouraged that James made early efforts to meet with environmental lobbyists in Washington. He hoped he could assure them that he wasn't against the environment, and perhaps set up a basis for ongoing communication. In mid-May of 1981, James met with a group of major environmentalist executives who presented him with ten proposals regarding Interior Department policies. They included items such as prohibition of oil drilling in marine sanctuaries, enforcement of strip mine rules, protection of wilderness areas, and policy changes on protecting endangered species. James surprised the men by actually agreeing with seven of the ten demands, yet immediately after the 90-minute meeting the leaders met with the press and issued a preprinted statement saying that they had irreconcilable differences.

Jay D. Hair, executive Vice-President of the National Wildlife Federation, was most vocal in his opposition: "The man is absolutely sincere. He just has a different vision of what stewardship of the public lands should be. We define stewardship as using our natural resources in ways that assume they can be restored over time. His definition is taking the resources and changing them irreversibly."

The press seemed intent on reporting every negative quote by his critics instead of the facts. It was hard for me to accept that anyone would intentionally distort the facts to hurt James or the President. *Why do they do it?* I cried out. Only after reading a major article in *Audubon* magazine did I begin to understand.

As I read the first half of the story, I saw that it was a factual presentation of his background. Then there was a subtle change in tone, and numerous accusations were leveled against him by unnamed "former colleagues" and "former high-ranking officials" in the Interior Department who ridiculed his philosophy. Because no names were attached to the charges, he could not face his accusers.

Nor was any attempt made to balance the viewpoints. The article carefully devised phrases calculated to alarm readers. It said that Mountain States Legal Foundation provided James with a "bully pulpit" to preach his "private enterprise gospel." He was a "servant of God" who was imposing his particular standards on an unwilling country. He was a "fox put in charge of the henhouse" and his department appointments were known as the "Rocky Mountains Mafia." The *Audubon* article (May 1981) concluded with these words:

> The environmental movement in America has its foundation in a powerful religious tradition, even though its modern-day proponents might be quite unaware of it. The environmentalists' sense of stewardship toward land and water and natural resources flows from identification with nature—the view, like that of Ralph Waldo Emerson, that the world is a mirror of the soul. In general this broad tradition has given rise to forms of belief in which a person's spiritual, physical, and even economic well-being are considered to derive from his rapport with all of creation, from being in tune with the infinite.

> At the other extreme is a more imperious, totally contradictory tradition. Based on a very literal interpretation of Scripture, this view holds that the Earth is merely a temporary way station on the road to eternal life. It is unimportant except as a place of testing to get into heaven. In this evil and dangerous world one's duty is to pass through unspotted by the surrounding corruption. The Earth was put here by the Lord for His people to subdue and to use for profitable purposes on their way to the hereafter.

Jim Watt is steeped in this latter tradition. It forms

the core of his life and values. Like the environmentalists, he talks at length about the need for stewardship and balance, but he is immersed in a religious tradition in which those words have a very different meaning. Although his opponents have criticized his words and his deeds, the real source of their objections springs from who he is.

This article, the meeting with environmental leaders, the National Wildlife Federation questionnaire, the continuing barrage of negative quotes began to convince me that there were two contradictory views. "You're on parallel tracks and you will never meet," I told James one night. "You worship the Creator; your opponents worship the creation." James' job was that of a steward, caring for the land and managing its resources for this and future generations. The goal of environmentalists was to preserve as much of the environment as possible, preferably totally undisturbed. People's needs were not part of their equation. When James saw that this difference was irreconcilable, he accepted it and stopped worrying about trying to please this special-interest group.

But the problem was even more serious for me. Not only were there opposing philosophies, but this was a real battle. There were several threats on James' life, and police security was required everywhere he went. The constant pressure caused me to be more intense in my morning prayer times. Often I claimed the promise of Psalm 138:7: "Though I am surrounded by troubles, you will bring me safely through them" (TLB). I would put James' name in there and pray, *Lord, though James walks through the midst of trouble, You have promised to preserve his life. Lord, You know he's in the midst of trouble. He isn't destroying Your creation. Their accusations are without foundation. Help him to get the facts out. Thank You for Your promise to defend him.*

It was on the road that I gained a new appreciation of our intimacy. It was one thing to stand beside my husband in the quiet privacy of our home, or in the banquet hall where everyone was cheering. It was quite another to stand with him in the face of hateful demonstrators. At many places we visited, demonstrators marched with signs like "Dump Watt," "Down with God, Up with Trees," "Dam Watt, Not Rivers," "Kill a Watt, Save a Tree." Some of the signs so blasphemed God that I couldn't even repeat them. They shouted insults and four-letter words, and I could feel the hatred directed at James.

One of the worst demonstrations was in Denver, where James' parents joined us for the American Mining Congress convention. He was scheduled to give a major address. His mother had called James several times to ask what he was doing to "make all those nice people angry. I thought I taught you how to be polite." she corrected him one evening.

"Mom, their minds are set. Nothing I can do would satisfy them."

"But James, if you'd just sit down and talk with them, you could get all these problems ironed out."

"Mom, I've tried. Just come to one of the events and see for yourself."

The convention was the first time they had seen James in his official role as Secretary of the Interior. They sat proudly next to me in the front row of the convention center. Behind us were 4000 delegates eager to hear James speak.

Shortly after we arrived through the service door, demonstrators in front of the building broke through police barricades into the hall and started slamming their placards on the floor-to-ceiling windows of the foyer. Their rhythmic banging and chants of "Dump Watt! Dump Watt!" reverberated through the convention hall and diverted attention from the platform where James was waiting to be introduced. I wondered how long the glass could resist such pounding before shattering into thousands of sharp pieces. Within a few minutes, police cleared the foyer, but the peace didn't last. The demonstrators moved around the building to a large maintenance door immediately behind the platform. Their pounding on the metal door made an even more disruptive noise, but this time the police did nothing to stop them.

Next to me, Mom looked perplexed. She turned and asked, "Is this what the demonstrations are like?" I told her this was typical. She shook her head and whispered, more to herself than to me, "He hasn't even spoken a word yet."

As James stood to speak, out of the corner of my eye I saw a well-dressed man stand and reach his hand inside his suit jacket. My heart jumped into my throat. *A demonstrator. He's got a gun!* There was no time to respond, and I knew it would be over in seconds. But instead of a gun, the young man pulled out a paper with a statement which he began to read loudly, to the consternation of everyone around him. A half-dozen other demonstrators now stood throughout the hall, shouting so that my husband was unable to begin his speech. *They have badges!* I noticed. *How did they get in here?*

Lord, I prayed, *please help James now. Show him what to do.* James stood at the podium, unwilling to signal any retreat. Then he spotted two television cameras and instructed the cameramen, "Go over there and take their pictures. All they want is to be on the evening news. Then we can get on with the program." One by one the demonstrators popped up and made their speeches, then were escorted from the hall.

One row behind us and across the aisle I noticed another protester, his eyes filled with anger, obviously biding his time. Impulsively I jumped up and yelled, "There's another one over here," pointing to the man. The cameras turned to film the man, who stood and read a statement.

As I sat back down, I noticed that one of the delegates, a broad-shouldered man who looked like a guard on a professional football team, stood up, removed his jacket, and rolled up his sleeves. He stepped into the aisle, grabbed one of the demonstrators by his ponytail and began to drag him down the aisle. The crowd erupted with a tremendous ovation for their fellow delegate's action as the police rushed in to separate the two.

It took 15 minutes for the intruders to be removed and for order to be restored in the hall before James could begin his speech. "If I did what these demonstrators wanted," he said before starting his prepared talk, "and locked up the nation's lands and deprived the country of needed energy resources and jobs, you folks would be the ones demonstrating and they would be cheering." The audience responded with a standing ovation.

James completed his speech, noting that the United States was critically dependent upon foreign sources for at least 22 of 36 minerals which are considered essential to the economic well-being of our nation. He again stated that there would be no mining in national parks, but insisted that mineral exploration and development needed to be encouraged on public lands not already declared off limits by law. The media chose to ignore his speech and instead showed the demonstrators on the evening news. As James hugged his parents before we boarded another plane, I sensed that they now had a new understanding of the battle he was in.

From that moment on, as we traveled, local law enforcement agencies increased personal protection forces everywhere we went. Often during his trips James would meet with local environmental groups. He found the regional representatives more reasonable and willing to constructively discuss various issues and concerns. But there were personal risks as occasionally environmental leaders used the meetings as a forum for vicious verbal attacks rather than an examination of the facts. One such meeting occurred in a Midwestern hotel.

We assembled in a bare meeting room. Not even a cloth was on the large folding table set up in the middle of the gray-green carpeted room. A dozen metal chairs surrounded the table, which contained two pitchers of ice water and several glasses. The only other pieces of furniture were a row of chairs against one of the bare white walls and a coatrack. Eight representatives of local environmental groups lined their chairs on one side of the table, and James sat opposite them. One of his aides, Roger Brown, sat at one end, where he set up a small tape recorder. I could feel the hostility as soon as I walked into the room, but I shook their hands as warmly as I could. I decided to sit about six feet behind my husband in one of the chairs that lined the wall.

It suddenly struck me that all eight men were wearing suits, which was unusual. Representatives of these organizations usually dressed casually. One man particularly caught my attention. He had on soft, glen plaid slacks with matching vest, but instead of a suit jacket he wore a bulky, black nylon windbreaker. I immediately wished that one of our security men had joined us in the room as they had requested. In a security briefing I had been warned that this type of nonconforming clothing could conceal a gun or knife. This man's eyes revealed a piercing hatred that made my knees wobble.

The man directly in front of James also took out a tape recorder and made the first statement. Rather than following the previously agreed-upon agenda, he began an intense diatribe against my husband. James tried to correct him when he quoted inaccurate information about policy, but the man wouldn't allow him to speak. When he was finished the man next to him spoke, and around the table they went, with each man making vicious verbal assaults against James.

I was stunned by the attack. It took a couple of minutes to recover and realize that as an intercessor I needed to absorb these blows for James. *Lord,* I prayed, *please soften the hearts of these men. Let them vent their anger so they can deal with the issue. And Lord, please help James to overlook the insults and respond appropriately to the issue.* Mentally, I pictured myself between James and his accusers, taking the abuse for him so he could concentrate on the facts.

As I prayed, I noticed that James' water glass was empty. I got up and reached for one of the pitchers in the center of the table to fill his glass. However, I now realized I couldn't just serve James. I had been taught as a girl that, if you served one person, of course you served them all. I started around the table. The first man I came to was the one in the black windbreaker. I asked him if he would like his glass refilled. He jumped back, startled because he had not expected the interruption. As I picked up his glass to fill it, I would just as soon have poured the water over his head. Instead, these words flashed into my mind: *A cup of cold water in the name of Christ.* I was humbled. *Oh, Lord, I was praying for these men, but my heart is also hard. Please forgive me.*

In a hostile situation, the Lord was asking me to show kindness. He wanted me to respond as Christ had in similar circumstances. I put down the first man's glass and picked up the next. With each glass I filled, I said to myself and to the Lord, *This is a cup of cold water in the name of Christ.*

It would have been nice to report that the meeting

improved after that. But it didn't. Even though it was agreed ahead of time that this would be a private meeting, the environmental group gave their account of it to the press, and the reaction in the papers against James was very negative. I realized that God expected me not only to intercede for James, but to be kind no matter how insulting or harsh the atmosphere. That lesson was tested many more times in subsequent meetings around the country. Sometimes I would emerge from those meetings drained as if I'd boxed 15 rounds, even though I never said a word.

The environmentalists had planned a media event for their final blow in the drive to force James from office. It was the delivery to Congress of more than one million signatures, gathered by the Sierra Club, demanding that James Watt be fired. The signatures, representing the largest citizens' petition ever presented to Congress, were delivered to House Speaker Tip O'Neill and California Senator Alan Cranston in mid-October. Said Cranston, "In thought, word and deed, Mr. Watt has played out his role as a puppet of the exploiters and destroyers. He represents a radical reversal of a long-standing bipartisan tradition of love and respect for the land."

In fact, James was improving every type of federal land in America. The policies he was implementing were the ones he and the President thought to be correct. Congress was supporting the changes by the budgetary process.

After the publicity from the Sierra Club drive, James met with his political team one Monday morning, as he always did, and told them, "We did not come here to be popular. We came here to make a difference. And when you make a difference, you will make waves." He said that the seas were going to get rougher, and anyone who wanted to leave should feel free to do so, and no one would say anything against him. "Don't stay here if you can't take the pressure, because there's going to be a lot more pressure in this job."

James received a flood of speaking requests from groups that wanted to hear exactly what this controversial figure had to say and learn what he was doing. Members of the Republican party liked what they heard, so much so that by the end of 1982 it was reported that James had raised more money for the party than anyone else with the exception of the President himself.

It was frustrating to me that, apart from these appearances, the public was unable to learn the truth. The press seemed unwilling to print it. Government funds could not be used for a campaign that might counterbalance the million-dollar publicity budgets of environmental groups.

Equally disturbing to me was an article from the *Milwaukee Journal* in July 1981: "Ultimately the major threat to Watt's stewardship may not come from environmental groups but from within the Republican Party. The Northeastern, conservation-oriented Republicans now shut out of the Reagan Administration will wait for a crucial mistake and then Watt's strength will be tested."

I had a new appreciation of the pressure on a public official who was at the mercy of public opinion he couldn't control. I was now convinced that what my husband often said was right. We *were* in a battle—a political and spiritual battle for the future of America. I prayed that he would not lose his courage.

CHAPTER SIX

RIDICULED!

It was a beautiful, clear, early June morning. The sun was promising a warm day, minus the humidity that would later make the city simmer. As I finished dressing, I hummed a little song of joy. As usual, James was already downstairs, spending a few quiet moments alone before the start of another hectic day.

I fastened a necklace and brushed my hair quickly before starting down the stairs. At the foot of the stairwell I looked into the living room and saw James, still in his pajamas, staring out the patio window. Usually by now he was in the shower. I could sense something was wrong. He turned around and I saw he was fighting tears.

"Honey, what's the matter?"

"Look at the paper," he said, pointing to the *Washington Post* that lay open to the editorial page on one of the wingback chairs. At the top of the page was an editorial cartoon, and as soon as I saw it, I felt as if a sword had been run through me.

The cartoonist, Herblock, had in his destructive style drawn an insulting cartoon titled "Onward Christian Soldier." It showed my husband, with buck teeth, marching with a poster which read, "Why save it? The End is Near." A bulldozer was in the background ravaging the land. A startled Uncle Sam looked on in disbelief. The cartoon was designed to ridicule my husband's religious commitment.

I was stunned. I slumped to the edge of the chair. *How could anyone so misrepresent my husband's Christian faith or the Interior policies?* It was totally contrary to the truth. Nothing he had said or done could even imply that he intended to destroy our land.

Moving slowly, James headed upstairs to dress. I wanted to hold him. To cry with him. But I was riveted to the chair. How could I possibly understand this hurt? I had seldom even been privately rebuffed for being a Christian. *That is a malicious twist, Lord. It's ridicule. Lord Jesus, help him to stand fast. Oh, help me to comfort him.*

It took James longer than usual to dress, and when he came back down for breakfast, he looked as though he'd been whipped. He ate his breakfast without a word, then picked up his briefcase and walked silently out the door. There was no cheery "Good-bye" or "I'll see you tonight" or "We'll get 'em today," that he usually gave when he left for work. He seemed like a man headed for his execution.

During the six months since his appointment by the President, James had repeatedly proclaimed that he was intellectually, emotionally, and spiritually prepared to handle this job. As I watched him leave and go to his car, I knew he hadn't anticipated an attack like this. The early months of James' term as Secretary of the Interior had been full of controversy. There were numerous tough decisions, and many of them were not popular. He had cut the Department's budget by 877 million dollars, increased involvement of private enterprise in providing services for people who visit our national parks, accelerated oil and gas leasing programs on the outer continental shelf, and, as directed by Congress, reduced federal regulation of the mining industry. James had handled all that controversy, and even seemed to thrive in spite of it. He had the ability to see the best in a negative situation.

But recently the media attacks had taken a new, more vicious approach. Rumors began to circulate around Washington that "James Watt, the Christian, was out to destroy the environment." He began getting strange questions at press conferences, such as "How do you define 'subdue the earth'?" and "How does the Lord's return affect your policies?'" James told me one evening, "I don't know how to handle those questions. Where do they get those ideas? I'm asking Doug to find out where they came from." Doug Baldwin was James' officer in charge of public affairs. If anyone could find out, he could.

Environmental groups and several congressional leaders were furious at James. "From all indications, the man in charge of protecting this country's resources is a zealot," said a spokesman for the Wilderness Society. Democratic Representative Phillip Burton of California called him the "environmentalists' nightmare" and said that the Reagan Administration had declared "unconditional war on our great natural resources."

Columnist Colman McCarthy of the *Washington Post* cynically portrayed James' religious convictions to mean public lands were under "divine mandate to be bulldozed, levelled, drilled, mined and leased down to the last holy square yard." This morning's cartoon graphically reiterated that distortion.

I couldn't help but cry out with the pain of it now as I sat in my rocking chair, trying to pray. *Were they ridiculing something they didn't understand? Or were they deliberately blaspheming against God?*

Many of the articles had caustically referred to James' "born again" or "charismatic" experience. I could still vividly recall that cold February night in 1964. He had come home from a Full Gospel Businessmen's meeting that I had encouraged him to attend. His face looked different—radiant and rested. He was never that relaxed after a full day working in Senator Milward Simpson's office.

Despite the late hour, James had wanted to tell me about the evening. He pulled off his tie, stretched out his six-foot-two frame on the floor and leaned back against the couch. I huddled close to him in my winter bathrobe. "It was rather confusing," he told me. "When I got to the hotel, there were hundreds of people, but many of them were women. Everyone was wearing long badges with the letters FGBMFI on them, and I didn't know what that meant. I finally asked one of the women where the Christian businessmen's meeting was, and she said to go right into the auditorium."

He proceeded to tell me about the meeting in the Statler Hilton Ballroom, attended by at least 2000 people. "I couldn't hear all they said, but one thing I did understand was that these men were telling success stories. Some told about going from poverty to financial success. Others told of marriages that had been restored. One young man told about a disease that was dramatically healed. In order to hear more, I moved toward the front."

One of the ushers stopped him and said it was full. If he would wait, they were setting up more chairs in back. Such instructions never seem to apply to my husband. He can go to a parking lot marked "Full" and find a parking space. He can go to a ball game that has been sold out for two weeks and get tickets. So in typical fashion he pushed on ahead and found a single seat in the third row.

"I sat down next to this little guy who had a large nose," he told me with a laugh. "Every time the speaker said something he liked, he'd say 'Hallelujah!' It was really distracting. Several times I turned and glared at him, but he just smiled at me and softly said, 'Praise Jesus.'

"Then a Baptist minister from Canada spoke. I can't remember what he said, but after he was finished they started to sing. The leader—his name was Demos Shakarian, a dairy farmer—interrupted the music and said, 'Just a minute. There is someone in this crowd who wants to know Jesus.' Lani, when he said that, my heart felt like someone had gripped it tight. My thought was, 'Do *I* know Jesus?'

"All my church activities kept running through my mind. I was born a Congregationalist. . .but do I know Jesus? I was active in the Presbyterian church. . .but do I know Jesus? I was chairman of the Social Concerns Committee at the Methodist Church. . .but do I know Jesus? I'm attending a Southern Baptist church . .but do I know Jesus?

"Demos asked all the Christians to close their eyes and pray. My heart was pounding. Then he asked those who would like to know Jesus to put up their hands. Inside my head I kept hearing, 'Do you know Jesus?' 'This is ridiculous,' I thought. 'Here I am a leader in the Republican party, a top assistant to a United States Senator, a loyal American, and active in the church. How can I admit I don't know the guy who started the Christian religion?' Then I remembered that Demos had said all Christians were to close their eyes. So I knew no one would see me.

"So I raised my hand.

"Then he said, 'Now those of you who have slipped up your hands, will you please stand up?' I can't believe it, Lani, but I stood up. And then he said, 'Those of you who are standing, please come forward.' That was so hard to do, especially the first step. But as soon as I took that step, I felt a warmth. It was like Jesus was walking with me. They led us in a short prayer, and I committed my life to Jesus Christ."

That was the beginning of his Christian commitment that was now being ridiculed. Almost immediately I had noticed changes in him. Not anything spectacular, for he had always been a moral, upright man. Rather, something was different on the inside, and he knew it. As a lawyer he went to the "books" to understand what had happened. He started reading the Bible at Genesis. One evening he popped the Bible shut with finality. "That's it!" he grinned. "I know what happened at the hotel. I've just read the story of Noah. In it God said He was grieved that He had made man. That word 'grieved' hit me. If God was grieved, then something had gone wrong with the man he created."

With that, James understood for the first time why it is crucial to know Jesus. Despite living a good, clean life, he saw that he, like everyone else, had grieved God by sin. In a way, Jesus' death is for today what the ark was for Noah—the only way. But the fact was settled: James was now under God's jurisdiction.

Like the lawyer he is, James approached the Christian faith by looking for evidence of its reality. He was particularly intrigued by the prayers he heard at a church we visited many Sunday evenings. Over the years of his church involvement, he had prayed and heard many prayers, but they were all very general—for things like the betterment of mankind and peace in the world. But these people prayed specifically and received specific answers. They asked God to heal a small boy of a ruptured eardrum, and the next day, when the doctor examined him, there was no infection or scar. They asked God to provide financial help for a filling station operator on the brink of bankruptcy. The next week the local banker who had repeatedly refused him a loan called to say he had changed his mind.

The evidence of God's power so overwhelmed James that one Sunday evening he opened himself and began to truly worship the Lord. In the following weeks and months he began to pray in the Spirit for specific areas in his own life, not just in church, but while driving a car, on the Senate floor, or before making a presentation before the Supreme Court.

Now, as Secretary of the Interior, James' faith remained an integral part of his life. Each morning before heading for the Department, he began his day by reading from a well-worn Bible. Then he would pray for his family and his work, often using several of the homemade banners that sat upright in a container in front of the fireplace. He liked the bold, bright lettering of promises like "The Lord shall fight for you and you shall hold your peace" and "I have called you into righteousness and I will hold your hand."

James had never been ashamed to let people know he was a Christian. *But now to be publicly maligned for Christianity — will it silence him?* Washington gossip columns had reported outrageous rumors that James Watt had banned coffee, tea, and cigarettes from executive offices, that he had made a new organizational chart for the Department with God on top and James Watt underneath, and that he had forbidden all female employees to wear slacks to work. We dismissed such stories for what they were—pure gossip with no basis in fact.

But it was the quote about the Lord's return that had

started this national uproar over his faith. Doug Baldwin had learned that James had made a remark at an orientation briefing to the House Interior and Insular Affairs Committee on February 5. The hearing was a courtesy to the House of Representatives following his confirmation by the Senate. It was several weeks later before the first references to the quote appeared in newspapers, and most articles failed to note where it was made, and none gave it in the proper context.

The now well-known quote had come in answer to a question by Congressman James Weaver of Oregon:

"I believe very strongly that we should not . . . use up all the oil that took nature a billion years to make in one century. We ought to leave a few drops of it for our children, their children. They are going to need it just to eat, not to drive around in gas-guzzling cars, just to produce the food they will need. I wonder if you agree, also, in the general statement that we should save some of our resources—I am not talking about scenic areas or preservation, but basic resources for our children. Not just gobble them all at once."

My husband answered, "Absolutely. That is the delicate balance the Secretary of the Interior must have, to be steward for the natural resources for this generation as well as future generations. I do not know how many future generations we can count on before the Lord returns. Whatever it is, we have to manage with a skill to leave the resources for future generations."

Congressman Weaver then asked the committee chairman if, "seeing the Secretary brought up the Lord," he might conclude with a story. The chairman, Morris Udall, granted permission. Weaver then told about a letter he received from a constituent that said, " 'Mr. Weaver, if the Lord wanted to leave the forest lands . . . in the way that we got them from Him . . . why did He send His only Son down to earth as a carpenter?' . . . .

That stumped us until one of my aides . . . said that the Lord Jesus before He determined His true mission spent 40 days and 40 nights in the wilderness." Everyone at the hearing laughed at the joke, then the questioning continued. While the questions to my husband were pointed, in no way did anyone at that hearing interpret James' comment as a personal mandate to ruin the environment.

This twist—that the Lord was coming soon, and therefore James would destroy the land—was picked up and accepted by much of the press and some members of Congress as fact, and as the basis of their opposition. Nothing could have been further from the truth, as the text of the statement clearly established. *And now this editorial cartoon, Father.* In my rocking chair, my Bible open on my lap, I cried out to God, *Help him. He's Your man. Your creation gives us beauty and resources. Your own Word teaches stewardship. Don't let him be distracted by these outrageous lies. Help him focus on his work today. Strengthen him.*

I doubled over with the pain of that awful cartoon. *Show me how to help my husband, Lord. He's never been so hurt by the press. I've seen him deal with attacks on his policies, but how can he answer the attacks on his faith? Please give him something to encourage him.*

Within a couple of hours I had an answer to this prayer. That morning happened to be the time of our weekly Cabinet wives' Bible study. Upstairs in the library of Fellowship House, I broke down as I shared with these women what had happened to my husband. Sallie Clingman hadn't seen the cartoon, but she shared with me from Psalm 62, which she thought was meant for James. Rarely has a Bible passage seemed more relevant. When I got home later that day, I wrote a note to James, encouraging him to read this Psalm, and laid it on his Bible.

The next morning James read those words penned by King David: "I stand silently before the Lord, waiting for him to rescue me. . . . " As he read those words, James sensed that God was speaking to him: "I will not rescue you. . . but I will defend you." When I came down to make breakfast, he told me with fresh enthusiasm about his prayer time. "God didn't say that He would rescue me. But He did say He would defend us. That probably means it's going to get worse, Babe." James left for work that morning with a spring in his step. Those words settled it. He would endure being ridiculed for his faith.

I wondered how God's defense would come. James was right about it getting worse. A month after the Herblock cartoon, he had a run-in at a subcommittee of the House Interior and Insular Affairs Committee. As I always did when James was called to testify, I prayed for him during the hearing, that he would have the wisdom to give satisfactory answers, that he would be courageous and not back down under attack, and that he would not compromise in presenting the President's program.

Amazingly, in light of their hearing in February, Congressman Weaver threw James' controversial quote back at him, and the following exchange took place:

"Mr. Secretary, several months ago you appeared before the Interior Committee and I asked you if we shouldn't leave a few of our resources for future generations. You responded that, yes, but that you didn't know how many future generations there might be. The Lord could come at any time. Are you approaching the environmental issue of surface mining [with] 'Why worry, the Lord's return is imminent?' "

"I am surprised at you, Congressman," James replied. "We are approaching the Office of Surface Mining in

accordance with the Act as passed by the Congress of the United States of America, and I have taken an oath to follow that law, and we will implement it, and I have asked repeatedly that we do it in concert with this committee, with the environmentalist groups, with the companies, and with the governors of the States. I am satisfied we will be successful in doing that. That is my mission. That is my purpose. And I would like to have your support in making this a reality."

"Is it possible that the return of the Lord, the imminent return of the Lord, is having anything to do with this?"

"I wasn't in Congress when it was passed, so you will have to—"

"What you are saying, I am asking, not what the law said. You have been quoted indirectly as saying that you're going to gut these laws by changing the regulations."

"Thank you, Congressman. I have never said that."

"I didn't say you said that. I said 'indirectly.' "

"That's why I say 'thank you,' because you have allowed me to say this: I am tired of people telling what I have said. I have never said that. My statement [today], and I think you were here when I read that, tells how we are committed to this Act. In private conversations with the chairman we have discussed this thoroughly. My religious freedom is guaranteed under the First Amendment. I don't think that it needs to be an issue of this hearing."

That exchange, the Herblock cartoon (and others like it), the misuse of his quote about the Lord's return, and the scare phrases about his faith's effect on Interior Department policy dramatically showed me that we were not just engaged in a political battle—we were also embroiled in a spiritual battle.

There were some interesting developments as a result

of that insight. The press was determined to continue making an issue of James' Christian faith. Because
of the distortions, James stiff-armed such questions
as "What do you think the Bible means when it says
to 'subdue the land'?" His standard response was, "I'm
not going to answer that. Next question."

James took the message of Psalm 62 seriously and
was determined that, if God had promised to defend
him, then he would not defend himself. James would
gladly defend the President's program. He would defend his own Interior Department policies. He would
defend his appointments and commissions. But he
would not defend himself. Newspaper columnists could
poke fun at him. Cartoonists could lampoon him. Environmental spokesmen could hold him up for ridicule.
James was determined to ignore them and concentrate
on the job that President Reagan had called him to
do.

*It's difficult, Lord, for me to watch this hounding go
unanswered. How can James bear it?* I lamented. At
those times it helped me to remember that Jesus Christ
suffered far more scorn and insult. He was even crowned
with thorns, scourged, and mocked. And during that
whole time He refused to answer the groundless charges
against Him.

One night James and I talked about how this controversy had affected him. "The way you face this
is being watched by many people," I told him. "Remember how the disciples all ran away when Christ was
arrested? That's why He warned us that any attack
on our faith is really an attack on Him. Jamie, I'm
praying that you will be immovable. It's one thing
for us to expect God to always be with us. But this is
the other side. Can we be bold and keep standing beside
Him?"

James was silent, considering what I'd said. Then he

answered, "Thanks for being my wife, Lani. My 'old wife' would have crumbled by now. Yes, we're going to be bold. We're going to stand. With God's help, that's where we're going to be."

But in the months ahead, both my faith and James' faith were to be severely tested.

CHAPTER SEVEN

READING THROUGH TEARS

I t was impossible for me to relax as I turned on the television set and waited for the interview with James on "Good Morning America," ABC's news and information program. Over the past two years, James had been interviewed countless times, and he was able to anticipate most questions. It always seemed like a contest. Even when presented with distorted facts, or attacked by accusations from unnamed sources, he was determined to zero in on the issues and present his and the President's message. In his mind, he remembered that he wasn't really speaking to the interviewer, but to the housewife fixing breakfast for her kids, the businessman knotting his tie before leaving for work, and the retired lady drinking her second cup of coffee. That's why he usually only accepted live programs—so that quotes couldn't be lifted out of context.

While Frank Gifford, substituting for regular host David Hartman, finished a news wrap-up, I prayed again that James would convey the right information, even if the questions were rude. After a series of commercials, Gifford opened this segment of the show by reporting on a public-opinion poll concerning the Reagan Administration and its policies. "As you would expect, the economy has been the major concern of almost everyone we talked to. But there are other issues that stir up strong feelings. One is the environment."

In a survey of 1000 people around the country, Gifford reported that 30 percent gave a favorable rating of President Reagan's handling of environmental issues, but that 60 percent rated him as fair or poor. "We also sent 'Good Morning America' camera crews all around the country to personally ask some of the same questions asked on the poll. . . . Here's what you told us."

The first respondent was a designer: "As far as the environment goes, he'd just as soon say let's use it, burn it out, and if it's not here 20 years from now, that's the problem of our younger generations."

A bookstore owner said, "To me, one of the most glaring weaknesses is Secretary Watt, who I find the least likeable character in the Administration."

My stomach began to churn as nearly every quote put down my husband. A college student said, "I think James Watt is a maniac who should be sent back to wherever he came from. I think taking someone who was a lawyer for an oil company and putting them in that department. . .was very, very insensitive."

"Fire Watt," said an accountant. "Get rid of him. I don't think that man knows what he's talking about."

How unfair, I thought, nearly in tears, as they finished the eight quotes. *If 30 percent of Americans supported the President's handling of the environment, couldn't they have shown at least one of those on film? Two of the quotes were neutral, the rest extremely degrading. How irresponsible to have one quote saying James was a lawyer for an oil company without explaining that this allegation was not true. He has never worked for an oil company.*

"Everywhere our crews went around the country, the response was similar," reported Joan Lunden, co-anchor with Gifford, back in the studio. "People have very strong opinions about the environment and about James Watt." On the screen behind her, my husband appeared on camera from Washington. "James Watt is with us this morning, and Steve Bell joins us too. Good morning, Mr. Watt."

I leaned forward a little more in my seat, wanting to catch every word. "You have now heard our poll results. Obviously . . . it's not the first time you've heard this kind of criticism. What do you think it is that arouses such passion in people about you and the job you've done?"

My husband smiled as he answered, "Well, Joan, if I believed what they've been led to believe, I would be for ousting Jim Watt too. America wouldn't tolerate that; Congress wouldn't permit it. Why, anybody that did the things I've been accused of would be out of Washington within five seconds. Fortunately, it's not true. We've got the federal lands—the national parks, the wildlife refuges, the public lands, the forests—in better shape today than they've been in for years. Much better than they were when we inherited them."

"Do you think perhaps you could serve the Administration better by tempering a bit more what you say?" asked Luden disparagingly.

"I have the ability to lay it out like it is, and I speak the truth as I see it, and people react different ways . . . . Yesterday I spent 3½ hours before a House Interior Committee and explained to them what we're doing. The most frequent reaction was, 'Gee, that's totally different than what we understood it to be.' The facts will catch up; I believe truth will prevail in the long run, if you can live through the short term."

Steve Bell broke in, "Let's put the verbal dexterity aside and get down to the critics' basic claim, which is that you're giving away public lands—that you've given away multiples by comparison to other recent administrations in only two years' time, and that it's all a ploy, in effect, for the benefit of big business."

I felt as though I'd been punched in the stomach. *What an insult! I can't believe this man is so brash. No Secretary can give away public land. Steve knows that. Lord, help James ignore the insult.*

"Well, of course, Steve, we haven't given anything away. First of all, we have made more oil and gas lands available from the lands that *are* available for leasing. There's no drilling or mining in the national parks, and in the wilderness we're not letting any drilling or oil activity. But in the multiple-use lands, we have accelerated greatly because we're consumer-oriented. But it's never given away."

"But federally owned coal sales are up eight times over the last two years under Carter," Lunden interjected.

"Yes...we're up eight times over what President Carter did, and not even half of what Secretary Udall did in 1968. So we've put more stringent environmental safeguards on everything we're doing than has ever been done before." James brought out a chart to show how the Democrats under Carter cut funding for national parks every single year. "We've doubled funding because we believe in parks."

Good for you! Use the charts. Then the audience will see at least one fact!

"You believe in the parks for what use?" Lunden demanded.

"For the people who can enjoy them now and in the years to come. We're preparing for the twenty-first century."

Realizing that James was scoring points, Steve Bell

took over. "Let's look ahead. William Turnage of the Wilderness Society says, and this is a quote, 'We think Watt is going to launch an all-out attack on public lands in 1983. They muzzled him before the election in '82. This will be his year.' "

Lord, why do they harass him like this? I prayed. *They say he's giving away public lands, that he's going to destroy our resources, that they muzzled him before the election. It's just not true. By using that accusing tone, they're influencing the audience to be outraged.*

But James laughed. "Turnage is the greatest PR guy. He can manipulate you, Steve, and others better than anybody else. His boss, Gaylord Nelson [former Senator from Wisconsin] . . . voted to cut funding for the parks every year during the Carter Administration. We've got the record; the facts are with us, the rhetoric's with them. . . . Things are better, the lands are better managed than they've ever been."

"But you talked about having the support of Congress," Bell challenged. "Congress has specifically—and the courts in several cases—have specifically blocked you from moves you tried to make in terms of selling land or opening it up for development by business."

He's encouraging the viewers to believe those allegations. He's not asking questions. He's using a fear tactic. He is condemning my husband based on inaccuracy rather than the facts. Father, help James to ignore it.

"To the contrary, Steve. I've had the votes, we've done most of this through the appropriations process, and the shrillest critic you can find you'll see voted for me when he got back to Washington, away from the TV cameras."

"All right, Mr. Watt. Thank you very much." Lunden back in the New York studio abruptly ended the interview.

As I switched off the television, tears started to flow.

I was so glad I hadn't gone to the studio this morning. I wouldn't have wanted them to see me cry. No matter what ABC thought about James, they should have at least accorded him the respect of his oath of office. *Go ahead and ask the tough questions. Put him on the spot and make him defend his policies. But you didn't have to insult him with false accusations before the entire nation. You try only to discredit. Do you ever report honestly, so the viewers know the facts?*

Above the television cabinet was a small, handwritten sign tacked to the wall. I couldn't read it clearly through my tears, but I knew what it said, for it represented the prayer I had prayed most frequently for James during the last two years. "Though I walk in the midst of trouble, Thou wilt revive me" (KJV). It was a passage from Psalm 138:7. Unable to move yet from my seat, I prayed, *Lord, my husband is walking through trouble again. Members of the media goad him like an animal. Lord, preserve his life. Revive him. Help him not to be discouraged by the insults. May he continue to focus on his job today at the Department.*

The sound of the patio door sliding open caused me to jump to my feet. James was walking into the living room to pick up some papers on his way to the office. I ran to him and put my arms around him. "Jamie, you won," I whispered. "But at what a price."

James gently held me at arm's length and looked at my tear-stained face. "Lani, why are you crying?" He didn't seem at all upset. Though concerned for me, he actually was cheerful.

"Their tone was insulting, yet you stayed so calm and collected. You smiled. You laughed. You gave the right answers. But it wasn't right for them to treat you so rudely."

He smiled and held me close, "That wasn't any different from many other interviews." Then he quickly grabbed his things and walked out the door. "I'll see you tonight," he said with a wave.

As soon as he left I sat in my rocking chair, and now the tears really flowed. James didn't even see how he'd been insulted. It took awhile for the sobs to decrease before I could focus my thoughts on the Lord for morning prayer. Then the phrase *Insults have broken my heart* came to my mind. I searched until I found where, in Psalm 69, David gave that great cry of distress, telling of the insults he had endured. He also prophesied about Christ's suffering and the fact that no one would give Him sympathy or comfort.

Lord, look at the insults. Slowly I reviewed the program in my mind and presented each insult to the Lord. *They didn't give a balanced sample of public opinion. He's been on other shows where they've taken a similar approach, but at least they showed a couple of people who supported what James was doing.* I thought through the questions, and particularly the accusation that James was giving away public property. As I presented those insults before the Lord, I cried again, feeling fully the anger and frustration of the experience. *I've got to resolve this. James needs a quiet home, and he needs me to have a quiet heart.*

The phone rang, and I got up to answer it. It was our son, Eric, and he could tell immediately that I'd been crying. "Eric, it was terrible this morning. They were so rude to your father when he was interviewed on 'Good Morning America.' "

"Wait a minute, Mom. Let me read you something. It's a poem by Kipling that I keep on my desk:

If you can keep your head when all about you
Are losing theirs and blaming it on you,
If you can trust yourself when all men doubt you,
But make allowance for their doubting too;
If you can wait and not be tired by waiting,

Or being lied about, don't deal in lies,
Or being hated, don't give way to hating,
And yet don't look too good, nor talk too wise...
Then,
Yours is the Earth and everything that's in it.

For a moment I couldn't say a word for the tears. Then I whispered into the phone, "But Eric, I fail on every line."

He was quiet for a moment. Then gently he said, "Mom, the Lord does not expect you always to win; but He expects you to never give up. He does not expect you always to be a proud example, but He does expect you to yield to Him in difficult situations."

Now I cried openly, but this time they were tears of cleansing. "Thank you, son. I needed to hear that." I could hear him choking back the tears too as he prayed for me, that the Lord would allow me to see His perspective in this hard situation.

When we hung up I returned to my rocking chair, remembering the truth that God honors a broken heart turned to Him. I knew again that I could come to Him with my broken heart, and that He would hear me and understand. In a sense I was suffering this insult for James. Maybe that's why I was reacting so deeply to the program. He hadn't had time to think about the tone of the questions. He was intent on presenting the President's program and showing what they had accomplished in the Department. My function as an intercessor was to absorb even the insults that James didn't have time to hear. It wasn't easy to stand between James and his problems, but it was good.

As often happened, it was the ultimate example that gave me perspective. I thought of Mary, the mother of Christ. How she must have suffered to hear the abuse hurled at her Son as He hung dying on the cross! Her heart was pierced through. The Bible speaks about knowing Christ, and that includes suffering. "That I might know Him," wrote the Apostle Paul to the Philippians, "and the power of His resurrection, and the fellowship of His sufferings, being made conformable unto His death" (KJV).

As a Christian, I wanted to be intimately acquainted with Christ. I could not choose to just identify with the power of His resurrection and avoid His sufferings. The two were inseparable as long as we lived on this earth. It was easy to look to Christ for the blessings He gave and the miracles He performed, while overlooking the fact that He was misunderstood by His own people, insulted by religious leaders, and mocked by the Roman soldiers. He was spit upon, scourged, beaten, and finally crucified. If we ever encountered similar situations, Christ had already prevailed and would give us His strength in the midst of the trial.

I bowed in my chair, and in submission I finally prayed, *Lord, we yield to the insults we deserve, and to those we don't. Please give us Your strength.*

It was much later than usual when I finished praying. But I felt refreshed. It was good that the tears were gone. James could come home to a wife who was at peace.

That evening as we talked over dinner, James admitted that he wondered about my reaction to the interview on "Good Morning America." "You know, you were right. They did insult me. They admitted they got a lot of phone calls complaining about their rudeness. But that's not important. No price is too great to serve the President. I will do *whatever* it takes to fulfill his program."

James ate quietly, then suddenly looked up at me. "I want you to make a big banner for me. I want you to hang it in the stairwell where I can see it every morning."

"What do you want on it?"

"I want it to read, in big bold letters, 'Whatever it takes.' "

James never begrudged the personal price he paid for his loyalty. His relations with the media seemed like a never-ending battle. Everywhere James traveled, he was followed by a mob of reporters. Often I was lost in the crowd, fighting just to avoid being trampled by the television cameramen. They admitted they wanted to be on hand when he spoke, just in case he committed that fatal mistake that would lead to his resignation.

As I accompanied him, or interceded for him at home, my prayer was that the truth would be known. Because the facts were so easily buried or distorted, it seemed that prayer was often not answered. But I persevered. *Lord, if for some reason my husband doesn't know the facts, make sure his men tell him. Don't let anyone hide something just to make him or one of his policies look good.* I knew James wanted the facts told, and I prayed that reporters would print the truth.

Reading newspaper clippings about James' work helped me to better understand the pressure he faced. My friends thought it was foolish, but it allowed me to know how to comfort him. I asked Doug Baldwin to let me read all the newspaper and magazine clips that he collected from around the country, even the worst ones that he kept from my husband. I read them all. I read through my tears when I saw my husband's name jeered in headlines like: "Secretary Watt: He Is Acting Like A Jerk". . ."Watt Strikes Out". . ." 'Wimp' Gave Us Reagan, But We Have Gorsuch, Watt". . ."Preserving Our Pollution". . ."Jim Watt Gets His, Or The Antelope's Revenge."

Even though James didn't see these stories, he felt the pressure they created:

Denver's own—no, make that Wyoming's own—
James G. Watt has the Interior Department by the
throat, and is squeezing. . . all this is like saying Attila
the Hun had an impact on Fifth Century Europe.[1]

I never tire of reading Washington stories about Gorsuch and Watt. They are governmental ogres, from
whose fangs drip the blood of innocents. . . . They are
far right zealots determined to sacrifice the health and
beauty of a nation on the altar of commerce.[2]

There are a lot of nice things about Watt and Gorsuch, but the nicest of all is this: it doesn't matter
whether they are in office or not. Howdy Doody could
be placed in charge of both agencies. Or, if Republicans
were the least bit serious about economizing, the posts
could be left vacant.[3]

One of Watt's problems is that he is one of only 23
Americans over 40 who was born in Wyoming, and stuff
like antelope and wide-open spaces bores him. What
we really need—and it seems to me the kind of project
our interior secretary could really get behind—is
something that reflects our heritage a little more accurately: A National Pollution Park.[4]

It was hard for me to understand why the media
would be so one-sided. Early in 1981 I learned a lesson
in news reporting when I suggested to James, "Since
you've scheduled a press conference tomorrow, surely
now the facts will get out."

"Don't count on it," he snapped.

"But if you tell them the facts, surely they have to
print them."

"Why don't you take the paint brush, Babe?" he answered. Translated, that meant, "Come and see for
yourself." The phrase originated from an argument we
had had over painting woodwork. James had learned
to hand me the brush for any touch-up work while the

surface was still wet. Then I couldn't complain, because I was responsible for the final result. In this case, taking the paint brush meant attending tomorrow's press conference.

The auditorium at the Department of the Interior was nearly full when I arrived. There were representatives from all the networks, the wire services, the Washington papers, the *New York Times* and *Los Angeles Times,* the *Wall Street Journal,* and several smaller newspapers and magazines. Each reporter had copies of two press releases—one announcing the appointment of a commission to study underpayment of mineral royalties on government lands, the other about a proposed five-year leasing program for offshore oil and gas.

Disdaining any formal introduction, James walked onstage and opened the meeting by introducing members of the oil royalty commission. He then invited questions about this one issue.

"How serious is the problem?" a reporter asked.

James invited the chairman of the new commission, Dr. David Linowes, to answer: "We estimate underpayment to be 7 to 10 percent of total collection. This year we will collect 4 billion dollars, next year 6 billion dollars."

After four or five more questions, a reporter called out, "Secretary Watt, you keep raising the eyebrows of concern of environmental groups. . ."

James interrupted. "Does your question deal with mineral royalties?"

"No, sir, it does not."

"May I ask you to hold that, please? In fact, why don't you hold that forever!" Everyone in the room roared with laugher. A few minutes later, James opened the meeting for general questions.

A young lady blurted out: "Are you going to quit your job?" Again everyone laughed.

"Boy, whatever happened to preliminaries?" James quipped. "Yes."

The press corps let out a collective gasp. The woman asked, "When?"

With a laugh, James answered, "That gets more specific. When my usefulness has expired." He ignored the follow-up question about what he meant by that statement.

The next few questions dealt with his conflict with environmentalist leaders. Then a reporter asked, "You describe President Reagan as your close soul-mate. You have testified to Congress concerning the coming of the Lord at any time. Can you tell us what President Reagan believes concerning this apocalyptic possibility?"

James quickly dismissed that with, "I choose not to answer that question."

Finally a few of the reporters began asking about the proposed offshore leases. In response to a question about whether the market could bear such an extensive program that would make a billion acres available for oil and gas exploration during the next five years, James replied, "We do not expect that a substantial portion of the area available will be leased on the first go-round." He also emphasized that the strictest environmental safeguards would be used. "The environmental risks from offshore oil and gas are considerably lower than the risks from foreign tankers carrying imported oil."

I was extremely curious to see how the newspapers and television networks would treat this news conference. They had all received the same information. Would they read it? Ignore it? Use it? How would their reports differ? The *Washington Post* headlined, "Watt Probes Oil 'Theft' on Indian Lands," but about half the story dealt with environmentalist attacks against James. The final paragraph was devoted to offshore leases.

Washington's other daily at the time, the *Star*, featured

those leases with the headline, "Watt Presses Plans to Auction Billion Acres at Sea for Drilling." It labeled the plan controversial because it was "too environmentally risky." But I couldn't find in the same article a description of the increased stringent environmental safeguards that the government had promised. And why did the plan become labeled "controversial"? I couldn't find anywhere in the article information about how this might lower the price of gasoline or lessen our 40 percent dependence on foreign crude oil. Those would be welcome facts to most Americans.

The *Wall Street Journal* concentrated on the threatened court interventions by states concerned about their shoreline and fishing areas. The article failed to make it clear that it was Interior Department policy to consult with the governors, and that modifications could be made not only for fisheries and whales, etc., but also for submarine lanes. There was no background information that would have explained that these leases were in federal waters, beyond the three-mile state-regulated waters, extending out to 200 miles. All those cartoons with derricks on the shores were misleading—except in California, where the state has 3000 wells of its own, many within sight of the coastline, which were not James' responsibility.

A lawyer was quoted by the *New York Times* as saying that the "program represents a tremendous giveaway of Federal lands with inadequate [safeguards] for environmental review or control." I reread the article but could find no explanation that this federal land is only *leased* for ten years, and is never sold. So it could not possibly be a giveaway. *Why did they print such things?*

The *Denver Post* reported that "some energy companies suggest it is too extensive," and said that they do not have the capacity to develop that many acres. However, there were no comments from companies who said they did have the capacity. Was it possible that the one company which complained publicly may have realized that its own reserves would be devalued if more oil was made available to the consumer?

The *Los Angeles Times* headline read, "Watt Rejects Environmentalists' Demands for His Resignation." The two announcements that were the purpose of the news conference were buried near the end of the article. That was better than NBC and CBS. Their reports didn't even mention the news items, but focused exclusively on the never-ending battle with environmentalists. Obviously they felt viewers weren't interested in an announcement that might lead to lower fuel prices. This could have been some good news, it seemed to me, for Americans who remembered sitting in long gasoline lines.

This experience of attending the news conference and then reading the clips in the following days led me to make two conclusions. First, each reporter at the press conference must have had his own view of what government officials should be doing, and his reporting reflected his view. I understood that, but I did not understand sensationalizing a topic and then insisting that the coverage was objective. Once, after a Senate committee hearing where a previously critical Senator had admitted that James was correct about an issue, my husband asked a network reporter, "You're going to have to show that my figures were correct, aren't you?" She just laughed, "Oh, that's old news now. It's no longer controversial."

The other conclusion was that I had to lower my expectations of the press. It was useless for me to be upset and frustrated. I couldn't call an editor or reporter and correct the record. For the most part, the facts were not going to be reported in a way that the truth would be evident.

In a private conversation with a media reporter, I

voiced these conclusions. "But Mrs. Watt, you must understand that we have to report what people say, regardless of whether it is a fact. We let the reader determine what is fact for himself."

"But how will the reader determine what is fact if only one side is given?" I protested. When she excused herself without further comment, I realized that maybe this was precisely the point.

I was told that special reporters had been assigned by national newspapers to "bring down Watt." As I read the clips about other Administration officials, I realized that the nation was suffering from misinformation. Public outcry from reading emotional headlines or accusations had blunted many of the Administration's thrusts for change.

The *Anchorage Daily News* noted in July, 1981, "On other matters . . . the Reagan administration has withdrawn from the kitchen when the stove got too hot. We wonder how much heat Mr. Watt can take." I had the same question. I was aware that some things are destroyed by extreme heat. Other things are tempered, gaining strength. I had used Carl Sandburg's line many times to describe James: "The fireborn are at home in fire." But I had to wonder how much longer that would hold true for him.

[1]*Denver Post*, June 6, 1982.
[2]Ibid.
[3]Ibid.
[4]*Rocky Mountain News*, August 3, 1982.

CHAPTER EIGHT

A BOLD STAND

With great fanfare, the bands began playing as Air Force One taxied up to the ramp at Andrews Air Force Base. Military escorts in full dress uniform rolled out a bright red carpet. Then the airplane doors opened and the President and Mrs. Reagan, weary but jubilant, waved to the hundreds of cheering spectators welcoming them home.

Briskly, the President worked his way down the line of Cabinet officers. From my perch in the bleachers I saw James shake hands with the President. Then President Reagan walked to the microphone and made a few remarks about the success of the European Economic Summit Conference.

When he finished, we were all swiftly escorted to our waiting cars. Police motorcycles, their lights flashing and sirens screaming, surrounded the Presidential motorcade as it sped down the parkway. More police blocked traffic along our route. James avoided motorcades whenever possible, but this evening I was grateful. We were already late for a dinner at the Canadian Embassy.

I mentally reviewed what I would wear for the formal dinner—a white faille sailor top over a black floor-length skirt. At our house we made the quick change of clothes. Back in the car I spread a little gloss on my lips and reflected on how energetic I felt in spite of the extensive round of social events we had already attended this week.

At the Embassy the butler escorted us across the white marble foyer into a salon, where guests were gaily chatting over cocktails. There was only time to meet a few people before Ambassador Gotlieb escorted me into the dining room.

Dinner conversation opened easily, with discussion focusing on the Tissot collection of prints on the wall. It was a series of beautiful yet simple drawings of women. Part of the main course included a traditional Canadian vegetable—fiddlehead ferns. They were little green spirals about the size of a quarter. I could imagine James at the next table, looking at them and asking, "What are these?" He was getting another education in international cuisine tonight.

Before dessert was served, talk shifted to a serious discussion about the latest conflict in the Middle East. Just a week earlier Israel had invaded Lebanon, initially for the stated purpose of removing PLO artillery from the border and creating a 25-mile buffer zone. But it quickly became apparent that Israel's intentions were far more ambitious as their army pushed toward Beirut in an all-out attempt to destroy the PLO as an effective military and political force.

There had been considerable consternation in the West. Many people felt that Israel's prime minister, Menachem Begin, had betrayed our President. Arab leaders were infuriated, feeling the United States was either powerless to stop the invasion or else tacitly supported it. There were calls by numerous politicians for sanctions against future arms shipments to Israel. Discussion at the table reflected that sentiment. All the men seemed to oppose Israel's latest actions.

After listening for some time, I finally interrupted. "Perhaps you should all know that I am one at this table who is a strong supporter of Israel." For a moment it was embarrassingly silent. Only then did I realize that I had intruded into an area where I had strong views but no foreign policy expertise. Senator Mark Hatfield of Oregon and I spent the rest of the dessert course discussing our divergent Biblical views of Israel.

Two days later we attended the Ambassador's Ball, sponsored by Bonds for Israel. The Washington Hilton ballroom was alive with more than a thousand formally dressed socialites. I was glad I could follow Claire Schweiker's advice about not needing a new formal gown for each social occasion. I wore the same dress I had worn to the Canadian Embassy.

It was exciting to be with James at events like this. He was so easily recognized in a crowd as he stood so tall with his bald head, thick glasses, and big smile. People always swarmed around him, asking to be introduced, seeking an autograph, wanting advice, or telling him how they admired his gutsy stands. He loved the crowd and responded with a quick smile and kind word for each person.

Cabinet members had discussed whether to attend the Bonds for Israel ball. Several stated their opinion that attending this dinner would make it look as though the President approved of Israel's actions. Yet we received no directive from the White House. My husband's decision to attend was based on our personal support for Israel. What good does it do to call yourself a nation's friend, James reasoned, if you don't stand by her when she's in trouble?

Israel's Ambassador to the United States, Moshe Arens, greeted us warmly at the door. Later, as the dinner began, he seated James next to him as the guest of honor, since he was the highest-ranking official there. In fact, he was the *only* Administration official there. James and Ambassador Arens had instant rapport. They discussed the energy program in America. "You realize that in the Camp David Accord, the United States promised to supply Israel with her energy needs if she were ever cut off from her supply of oil," said James. "One of the President's policies has been to expand the exploration and development of energy resources in the United States. That is why we've sold leases to drill for oil on the outer continental shelf. But frankly, we aren't getting sufficient support for that policy."

The Ambassador frowned and said, "Well, the Jewish community is supporting you, aren't they?"

"No, they really aren't. Rudy doesn't even support me," James said, pointing to Senator Rudy Boschwitz of Minnesota, who was sitting across the table.

The Senator was now leaning forward, listening intently. "Well, Jim, I've never opposed you on anything."

"That's true. But you've never supported me, either. We've had some support from conservatives in the Jewish community. But the liberals have not spoken up and given any real support."

We felt very good about that evening and the new acquaintances we had made. The *Washington Post* featured a picture of James and Ambassador Arens on the social page. The next morning at the office, James dictated a letter, as he often does after such a function. It is his practice to thank the hosts and perhaps reiterate the subject of discussion and affirm any actions he has promised to take. So he wrote to Ambassador Arens, titling it "A Personal Communication" on the top of the letter:

I appreciate the opportunity of discussing with you the need for a strong, energy self-reliant America. If we do not reduce America's dependency upon foreign crude energy, there is great risk that in future years America will be prevented from being the strong protector and friend of Israel that we are and want to be.

If the friends of Israel here in the United States really are concerned about the future of Israel, I believe they will aggressively support the Reagan Administration's efforts to develop the abundant energy wealth of America in a phased, orderly and environmentally sound way. If the liberals of the Jewish community join with the other liberals of this Nation to oppose these efforts, they will weaken our ability to be a good friend of Israel. Your supporters in America need to know these facts.

I look forward to opportunities to speak to groups of your supporters in this Nation so that I might share with them the truth of what this Administration is trying to do for America and the free world.

A copy of the letter was sent to Senator Boschwitz. The letter was also distributed to several publications, including *Conservative Digest* and *Washington Times*, who printed it without adverse response.

Soon afterward speaking engagements were arranged for James before the B'nai B'rith's Anti-Defamation League in New York and the American Jewish Committee in Washington. James also mentioned the letter openly in several speeches.

Five weeks after the banquet, we were shocked to open the *Washington Post* to find the story of James' letter along with reaction from liberal Jewish leaders who demanded my husband's resignation. Some even called his statements a reflection of bigotry.

"First of all, I don't like being appealed to as a Jew on an issue that is essentially of concern to all Americans," said Rabbi Alexander Schindler, president

of the Union of American Hebrew Congregations. David
Saperstein, head of the Interfaith Coalition on Energy,
said, "I find it politically and morally offensive. I hear
a veiled threat that the Administration might cut back
its support for Israel if Jewish liberals do not remain quiet
about energy policies, even if they think these policies
are bad for America and bad for humankind." About
the only positive comment in the *Post* article was the
final paragraph, a quote from Senator Boschwitz, who
said, "It's a free country. He can write a letter to anybody
he wants."

Our personal and public support for Israel was being
distorted; now James was being called anti-Semitic and
a bigot! However, my main concern was not that James
might lose his job over this issue. We had been through
so many crises that perhaps I was learning to live with
the continuing threat of James leaving the Cabinet. It
seemed like a broken record; every time James said or
did something remotely controversial, it was cause to
demand his resignation. But I was concerned that we
not offend the Jewish people. So I faced it matter-of-
factly.

*Lord, it does not matter if the Jewish people ever
understand that we are irrevocably committed to them.
We are. Therefore, Lord, we ask to find favor with
You. In Your mercy, please forgive any offense. If,
for our commitment to Israel, we are misunderstood
and forced to leave this office, we will go. We want
to honor You and Your people. Make of this whatever
You will.*

The results of the Jewish controversy were very
interesting, and totally unpredictable. James and Ambassador Arens became friends. He invited us to a
special dinner at the Embassy on the occasion of
the visit of Israel's President Navon. As we drove
into the Embassy compound, we noted the increased

number of security guards who surrounded the heads of state and dignitaries.

We were whisked into the Embassy and found that about 40 people were invited to this particular dinner. They included Israeli President Navon and several of the men traveling with him, as well as some prominent leaders from the American Jewish community. Representing our Administration were Vice-President Bush and his wife, the Secretary of State and his wife, the Deputy Secretary of State and his wife, the Assistant Secretary for Middle East Affairs and his wife, and the Ambassador to the United Nations and her husband. I couldn't help noticing several quizzical looks as we walked into the room. They had to wonder why the Secretary of the Interior had been invited, because it made no political sense. I was honored that the nation of Israel would consider James such a good friend.

Dinner was festive, and my special privilege was to be seated to the right of Ambassador Arens. President Navon spoke eloquently of Israel and America. Our Vice-President responded warmly and graciously. At the close of dinner, over coffee, the Ambassador leaned over to me with a twinkle in his eyes and said, "I appreciated your husband's comments tonight. But please tell him not to send me a letter!"

Shortly thereafter Moshe Arens was promoted by Israel's Prime Minister Begin to Minister of Defense. When he returned to the United States in his new capacity, along with Foreign Minister Shamir, James was again invited to the Embassy, this time for a black tie stag dinner. Among the guests were several Congressmen and Senators who had attacked James because of his letter. James was honored to sit at the head table of eight, along with Secretary of State George Shultz and the two ministers from Israel—Arens, his friend, and Shamir, who later became Prime Minister.

Another result was that James and I were invited to spend four days meeting with members of the Jewish community in California. One of the stops was at the Simon Wiesenthal Holocaust Memorial Center in Los Angeles. Walking through that museum, for the first time we were graphically exposed to the full horror of the Nazi holocaust. Six stark black granite pillars, their tops symbolically jagged, stood at the entrance, along with a flame burning in honor of death camp victims.

Inside the building, we first saw drawings by Wiesenthal while he was a Nazi prisoner, including a rendition of a guard tower with walls formed of human skulls. Wiesenthal survived his internment and spent the postwar years hunting Nazi war criminals and bringing them to justice. Along one of the walls was a display showing the roots of anti-Semitism and the Jewish resistance movement. German children were systematically taught to hate Jewish people. The children were taught that these people were inferior and needed to be isolated in order to maintain and further develop a perfect race.

My heart was filled with shame as I viewed objects like a lampshade made from human skin and a scale model of the Auschwitz death camp. *How could human beings perform such atrocities? It happened because a whole nation was silent. The preachers in Germany's pulpits did not denounce the action. The intellectual and media leaders did not cry out in objection. They were silent.*

Near the end of the tour we were confronted by a large black-and-white photo of a gaunt survivor, standing at the fence of one of the concentration camps, pointing his bony finger to the leaders of the world in that day. The words under the picture seared our minds:

Here is to the world that did not care—
those who had ears but would not hear,
those who had eyes but would not see,
[those who had mouths but would not speak,]
those who had hands, but would not act.
And the few saints among them
                              who cared
                              who bled
                              who suffered.

We stood hand in hand before that haunting figure and dedicated our lives before God to *never be silent* in the battle for political liberty and spiritual freedom. The horror of the Holocaust was that because these people were Jews, they were marked for extermination. Not only was this historically and socially unique, it was frightening. Would there be another time when some are hunted down because they are distinguishable?

Since my youthful days as a believer, I had kept a special place in my heart for the Jewish people. The visit to the Holocaust Center dramatically enlarged it. In response, I wanted to honor the Jewish people today. I wanted to encourage them with kindness. I wanted to always thank them for the preservation of the Scriptures. And I wanted to live among them as a "righteous Gentile," even though many of them despised my husband. I kept thinking: To whom much hatred was shown, surely much love must be given.

To cement my commitment, I wanted to do something tangible. I was made aware that a United States Living Holocaust Memorial Center was being developed in Washington under the auspices of the Department of the Interior. Buildings and land had been dedicated near the Mall to house the Center. But millions of dollars still needed to be raised to meet the requirements for continued Congressional support. I offered to sponsor a showing at the White House of a documentary film called "To Bear Witness"—a moving film showing the reunion of death camp survivors and Allied liberators.

We sent out invitations to Jewish leaders and evangelical Christians across the nation. There were some who suggested that Jews and Christians might not be able to watch this film together because of the emotions and memories it evoked. But the auditorium was filled and we were deeply moved by the presence of survivors and liberators who viewed the film with us. Many saw how valuable a memorial about those involved in the Holocaust could be. The younger generation, who do not know its history, have never had the opportunity to learn from the remembrance.

At another meeting for installation of Holocaust Memorial Council members, we met Dr. Elie Wiesel, chairman of the Memorial and himself a survivor of the death camps. Nothing prepared James and me for meeting one who has survived such atrocity. He had suffered death from the hands of man, and lived. We struggled with our emotions and found it difficult to speak. To explain the impact of our meeting to him, I shared this story, told by a visitor to an underground church behind the Iron Curtain.

A pastor was returning to his church after years of torture and deprivation in a Communist prison. When he entered the back of the room, the singing stopped. None would have questioned the silence, for his physical appearance was appalling—pitiful. With barely the strength to maneuver to the front, the pastor turned to face the crowd. The silence deepened. No one moved. In suffering sentences, he greeted his flock and shared how Christ had strengthened him, and enabled him to endure. He thanked them for their prayers.

Exhausted, the pastor concluded and painfully shuffled his way to the exit. The continued silence was embarrassing to the visitor. There had been no welcome.

Hyman Bookbinder, Leilani and James, Elie Wiesel

No sound. No applause. Yet their faces were soaked with tears. At the appropriate time, the visitor asked why the congregation had not responded or even acknowledged the presence of the pastor. With tears continuing to flow, the hushed answer came, "What does one say in the presence of someone who has suffered so much?"

When Dr. Wiesel expressed his gratitude for the role the Department of the Interior was playing in providing this living memorial to the Holocaust, James said it seemed as if it were so little to do. As we parted, I could only say to Dr. Wiesel, "In the presence of one who has suffered so much, what can I say?" There were tears in our eyes as the door of the elevator closed.

• • •

When it came to speaking out about the moral problems of *our* nation, what could I do? I had not been aware of my own apathy, but when I saw the pictures of the stacks of bodies waiting to go into the Nazi ovens, I was hit forcefully with this thought: Isn't that similar to the stacks of aborted babies in plastic bags, waiting to go into the garbage? My silence on this issue really wasn't any different from the silence of church members in the 1930s and '40s in Germany. Silence almost destroyed a race of people; silence was now destroying 1½ million unborn babies a year. Both were murdered. I could not in good conscience condemn the former while ignoring the latter. Both involved a similar moral issue: How do I value innocent life?

I hadn't always felt so strongly. In fact for years I was unaware of the abortion question. It certainly wasn't an issue I had faced in high school or college. During my illness, I realized that I didn't have the strength to carry a child if I accidentally became pregnant. James and I sat on the bed talking about it one night, and he disagreed with me. He argued that if I became pregnant, I had no right to destroy a life.

The change in my thinking came when I realized that abortion was selfish, as if I were more important than life in my womb. It was an unwillingness to give up my convenience or my health for the benefit of another human being. God values all life. I needed to revamp my thinking.

The first time I really put that conviction on the line was at a social gathering of Administration wives. One of the women approached each of us individually and asked us to work with her in favor of abortion. As politely as I could, I answered, "First, we're going to be miles apart on this issue. I couldn't support you because I don't believe in your cause. To me, abortion is murder. I won't compromise on that. Second, even if I did agree with you, I couldn't join you because part of the President's agenda is to stop abortion. Since my husband is in his Cabinet, I don't think it would be right to work against the President's stated policy."

It was a significant moment for me because in earlier years I would never have taken such a public stand on any issue. I would have done anything to avoid stating my opposing view.

My husband was also becoming even bolder. Whatever the price, James wanted to speak out about the wrongs in America. He believed it was wrong for us to see our country moving toward socialism and not say anything about it. It was wrong to view the moral decay in our nation and remain silent.

In August of 1983 James delivered a speech to the General Council of the Assemblies of God in Anaheim, California. More than 3000 pastors and their wives from across the nation had gathered for this special breakfast to hear Pat Boone sing and James speak. At the head table I picked at my food, thinking again about this speech over which James had labored so long. This was not an ordinary political talk. We had discussed his message and we knew that this was a speech that could cost James his job. But even if it did lead to his resignation, there were issues that had to be addressed, whatever the cost.

Warm applause greeted James upon his introduction. "Thank you for the prayer support you have given to my wife and me. We feel that support and are grateful for it." Briefly he reviewed a few of the results from his nearly three years of work as Secretary of the Interior.

"As important as these responsibilities are, there is yet a more basic battle," James said, launching quickly into his main theme for the morning. "The real struggle . . . is over the form of government under which we will live . . . and pass on to those of the twenty-first century. Will it be a government that recognizes the dignity of the individual? Or will it be a government that elevates the institutions of a centralized authority above the rights of individual persons?"

James was in full stride, his arms gesturing, his fingers tense as he physically emphasized each point. He talked about the Holocaust and its lessons for us today. "The apathy and noninvolvement of the 'good people'—the church people—in the Nazi government activities of the 1930s made it easy not to smell the burning stench of human flesh in the 1940s. They lived in a town nearby, but they did not get involved to stop Auschwitz.

"And yet today, here in America, we see millions of Americans doing nothing about forces mounting in this land to deny us our life, our hopes, and our dreams.

What is mankind without political liberty and spiritual freedom?

"While we must be indignant about the inhumane, the diabolical action of Hitler, we in America today are denying life to 1½ million aborted babies each year. Oh, there are a few people who protest, a few people who try to change the law, a few people who march and write letters. But where is the voice of the Christian church? Where is the Jewish community? What are the silent people doing while this destruction of human life is carried out? It is murder. Let's call it murder."

I could see over to one side several reporters scribbling notes. That quote would almost certainly cause problems. But James was talking to our denomination's ministers. Silence was the issue. This was a message that needed to be declared. People needed to hear—to be warned. These ministers had to help motivate their congregations to get involved in the crucial social and political issues of the day. To preach against it was not enough.

"There are other issues in America where we see millions of silent people living in the towns nearby— not getting involved, not being committed, not standing for what is right. Most Americans are too busy to be concerned. We don't serve on our school boards, nor do we vote in the school board elections. . . .

"Today, America is confronted with yet another controversy that threatens our very existence—the nuclear freeze movement. The free people of the world do have an enemy—Communism. Many argue that the Communists don't seek to dominate and control the world. They argue that the Communist leaders want peace and can be reasoned with. The facts are to the contrary.

"The spokesmen of the present nuclear freeze movement have failed to review history. In 1939 there was only one Communist country—Russia—accounting for about 7 percent of the earth's population. Today Communist governments control more than a third of the world's population. In spite of these historical facts, respected spokesmen call for a nuclear freeze that would give Communist forces throughout the world a clear advantage. The proper conclusion, as seen from my perspective, is very clear. We must champion peace. And peace only comes with strength. We must never allow this great stronghold of spiritual freedom to agree to a freeze of its military capabilities at the level of inferiority."

Applause interrupted the talk again. It seemed to me that the ministers were agreeing on each of the points. I hoped this would be more than just an emotional response—rather, that it would be a commitment by these influential men to speak out.

"It is wrong for the Jews and Christians of America to stay out of political issues. We must get involved. We must not abandon those principles which are based on absolutes. There *are* absolutes in this world. And to deny that is to deny God. Without God, this nation cannot and will not survive, nor does it deserve to.

"The worst option available to America is noninvolvement by the spiritually inclined. For all legislation is based on moral values, and moral values should be weighed by the fundamental teachings of the religious perspective. To pretend that you may not mix religious and political activities is a hypocrisy that can no longer be afforded in this country."

The men and women stood as one to applaud the stern message. Many came behind the stage to shake James' hand. One handed him a letter; many wanted autographs. The crush was so great that we could barely move. The ministers thanked him for pricking their

consciences and charging them to find a way to get their people involved in citizenship. Here the message was received. Later, through the distorted news coverage, many would reject it. This was not a Department of the Interior policy speech. But James was determined that he would not be silent on the apathy he saw in America. *Silence is the issue. And often those who provoke the conscience are silenced. O Lord, help us to keep taking a bold stand.*

CHAPTER NINE

WHY IS YOUR HUSBAND SO CONTROVERSIAL?

At the southwest gate onto the White House grounds, the guard asked for identification. After examining my driver's license, he waved Ralph onto the long, curving driveway. Gold-braided guards helped me from the car under the portico entrance.

As I walked up the marble steps, I could hear the musical strains of a string quartet. At the head of the stairs another military aide escorted me into the State Dining Room, where guests were being served their choice of cranberry juice, Perrier water, or wine. This was the annual luncheon for Senate wives, and each Cabinet member's wife was hosting a table. I had just accepted a glass of cranberry juice when I spotted Secretary Pierce's wife, Barbara, across the room. Momentarily forgetting the other guests, we threw our arms around each other in greeting and enjoyed a warm visit. She was so seldom able to be with us that I cherished each time we had together.

When all the women had arrived, we were escorted

into the Blue Room where Nancy Reagan gave each of us a warm welcome. It had been just two weeks since the Beach Boys controversy, but my heart was at ease. It was easy to talk with her and, of course, the issue was never raised. The hurt I had felt was gone. *Wait. It will be better than all your planning.* Whatever that meant, it brought me peace for now. I was almost glad I couldn't see into the future.

From the Blue Room receiving line, we were led into the East Room. Round tables for eight were covered with sky-blue tablecloths. On each of the red-white-and-gold Reagan china plates was a white linen napkin, a name card, and a gift almost too lovely to open. Each of the favors contained an engraved pen. In the upper left-hand corner of each place setting was a menu card.

We lingered over each course: jellied consomme with sesame seed twists, Gruyere cheese souffle covered with Chesapeake crab sauce, and endive watercress salad. As we enjoyed a dessert of spring sorbet and petits fours, one of the women at my table leaned toward me and said, "I hope you don't mind my asking, Mrs. Watt. But why is your husband so controversial?"

As often as I had been asked the question, it still stung. *Will that impression of him always stick?* "I think it has to do with the nature of his job," I answered quickly, disguising my real feelings. "No matter who is Secretary of the Interior, he has to balance conflicting responsibilities that Congress has mandated by law."

"Like what?"

"Well, he's chief park ranger and chief coal miner. He's chief wildlife ranger and chief driller for oil and gas. He's chief protector of endangered species and chief dam builder. And he's chief Indian!"

Several of the ladies were listening and laughed at my joke, which was actually just the way James often described his job in speeches. But my questioner wasn't satisfied. "Then why haven't we heard of any other secretaries of the interior? Why is your husband always in trouble with the White House and the press?"

It was not pleasant confronting the misinformation. I wanted to be natural and light, but instead my voice tightened. "The President has asked my husband to change the direction of the Department. They believe there needs to be a balance between preservation and development. Bringing that balance has caused controversy."

"And, if you'll forgive me, Mrs. Watt, isn't it also your husband's style?"

I took a deep breath and began to speak more softly, deciding that these women should hear a more personal observation. I put some sparkle in my voice. "I've got a great answer for that question. Shall I tell you?" Several nodded their interest, so I asked, "How many of you have teenagers you wish you could understand?"

I saw a couple of knowing smiles, but I didn't wait for answers. Turning over the menu card, I drew a large square on it with my new pen. With two additional lines, I divided the square into four quadrants. "If my husband's critics had known this, they would have changed their tactics. Our family attended a seminar, taught by our friend Don Thoren, called 'Interpersonal Effectiveness.' What we learned saved us from innumerable fights. It was the turning point for me in understanding my husband's personality *and* myself."

As I talked, I wrote a word in each quadrant. In the upper left I wrote "analytical." In the upper right was the word "driver." "Expressive" was under "driver" and the last box said "amiable." I turned the paper for all to see.

LESS RESPONSIVE

- Reserved, unresponsive, poker face
- Actions cautious or careful, wants facts and details
- Eye contact infrequent while listening
- Eyes harsh, severe or serious
- Limited use of hands, clenched tightly, folded or pointed
- Limited personal feelings, story telling or small talk
- Preoccupied or vigilant

MORE ASSERTIVE

- Emphasizes ideas by tone change
- Expression aggressive or dominant
- Quick, clear or fast paced
- Firm handshake
- Made statements more often than asked questions
- Let one know what was wanted
- Tended to lean forward to make a point

	LESS RESPONSIVE	
LESS ASSERTIVE	ANALYTICAL STYLE	DRIVING STYLE	MORE ASSERTIVE
	AMIABLE STYLE	EXPRESSIVE STYLE	
	MORE RESPONSIVE	

LESS ASSERTIVE

- Few uses of voice to emphasize ideas
- Expressions and posture quiet and submissive
- Deliberate, studied or slow in speech
- Indifferent handshake
- Asked questions more often than made statements
- Vague, unclear about what was wanted
- Tended to lean backwards

MORE RESPONSIVE

- Animated, uses facial expressions, smiles, nods, frowns
- Actions open or eager, little effort to push for facts
- Eye contact frequent while listening
- Friendly gaze
- Hands free, palms up, open
- Friendly gestures
- Shared personal feelings
- Attentive, responsive, enjoyed the relationship

"There are four styles of personality. We all have one developed more than the other, a fact that becomes obvious in almost every group. All styles are necessary to get the best work done, and no style is right or best." I emphasized that point: necessary and neutral.

"The seminar we attended was designed for salesmen, to help them spot the personality style of a customer and adjust the sales pitch accordingly. You can see what a different approach you'd make to sell something to someone who wants details about how it works, versus someone who only wants to know *if* it works.

"I'll show how this works in my family. Our son would dominate a dinner conversation with every play of a soccer game. Our daughter would soon tune him out and James would say repeatedly, 'You don't need to tell us every move.' With the temperature rising, I'd try to make peace between father and son, while trying to include our daughter. The meal was a hassle."

"Sounds like my family!" said one of the women.

"How do you know which personality you are?" asked another.

"We took a short test. But for our purposes today, let's just suppose there is a job to be done around the house." I pointed to the chart. "The analytical thinks, 'I'd better be sure this is the best way' and doesn't want to make quick decisions. A driver looks at the known options and thinks, 'That's it. Just do it. Be finished.' The amiable hesitates and thinks, 'What if this isn't right? We don't want to offend anyone.' The expressive thinks, 'Let's think of some fun way we can all do this together.' "

"That describes my son exactly!" laughed the tiny blonde. "He's always trying to get several of his friends to do the chores with him."

"This seminar was so helpful to our family because we began to understand how to communicate with each other. The results of the test showed that our daughter was a driver. That meant, among other things, that long discussions would bore her; she only wanted to hear the bottom line. Our son, on the other hand, was an expressive. He loved all the excitement of new experiences and all the details. Of course, the young people change some as they mature."

"And mother was an amiable," another woman interjected.

"That's right!" I laughed. "I need everything to be calm. Can you imagine me in all the controversy surrounding my husband? I don't like conflict. When an amiable is hassled, he gives up ground just to keep the peace. An amiable wants to be liked, so he makes concessions. Now imagine how someone of my personality would fare with the conflict that my husband faces."

Pointing to the chart, I asked, "Can you guess what personality style my husband has?"

The woman in a striped blouse pointed quickly to "driver." With a grin she said, "It even sounds like him."

"That's right. All these titles describe the person fairly well. When the heat is on, a driver refuses to change if he believes he's made a good decision. He just keeps moving ahead. Drivers make good combat leaders. They say 'Charge!' in the face of attack. The amiable says, 'Retreat and regroup.' If the driver is pushed to the extreme, he can walk away and never have to give in. That's why personal insults or media pressure never intimidate my husband. He just keeps going."

I put down my pen. "So there you have it—the real James Watt." As I finished, entertainment by the Young Musicians Foundation of California was introduced. The young artists gave a brilliant performance of chamber music. After the program, Mrs. Reagan thanked the musicians and we all rose with her as the luncheon came to an end.

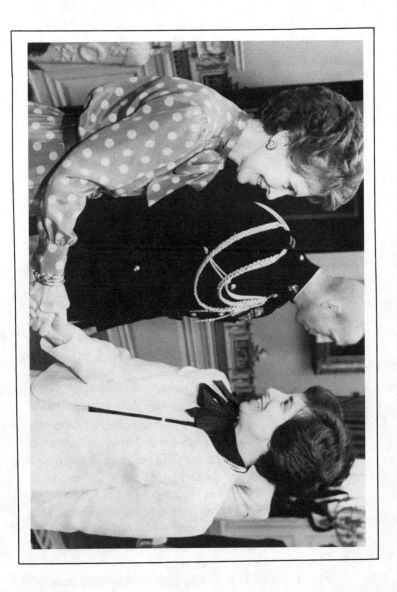

One of the women who had sat quietly during our conversation tapped me on the arm. "Thanks for explaining your husband's personality. I just want you to know that I've been praying for you. I appreciate the Christian stand you and your husband have taken." As I walked down to my car, I thanked God for her and many others who had let James and me know that they were praying for us. I also thanked God again for Don Thoren, who taught me how to deal with James' strengths, and showed me that it was all right to be the amiable one in our family.

●   ●   ●

The nighttime reflection on the wet Washington boulevards created an unending mural of light. As I stared toward the Capitol through the rain-streaked windshield of my husband's official car, my mind filled with anxious thoughts and prayers for the evening's reception. James had called earlier in the afternoon to warn me that we might receive a chilly welcome, and he gave me the option of staying home.

James was embroiled in controversy again, this time because of an overeager public relations man who was promoting my husband's appearance on a television program called "Conservative Counterpoint." The press release had erroneously claimed that James Watt wanted to abolish Indian reservations. The program drew record ratings, but the viewers didn't hear James say any such thing. In fact, there was nothing said that he hadn't already stated publicly on several other occasions. The press release was recalled, and UPI ran a correction on their story and apologized for not checking their facts. But the damage had been done.

"We have tremendous problems on the reservations," said James in answer to a question about policy for

Indian country. "I frequently talk about it by telling people if you want an example of the failure of socialism, don't go to Russia, go to an American Indian reservation."

This statement had been made by James in every speech about Indians across the country. He had picked up the language from the Indians themselves. The tribal chiefs saw the videotape, and their concensus was, "What's wrong with that?" Lawyers for the Indians— my husband called them professional redskins—whipped up the trouble.

James had gone on to say, "Every social problem is exaggerated because of socialistic government policies on the Indian reservations. They have the highest divorce rate, highest drug rate, highest alcoholism rate, highest unemployment rate, highest social diseases . . . because the people have been trained through 100 years of government oppression to look to the government as the creator, as the provider, as the supplier, and they've not been trained to use the initiative to integrate into the American system . . . . We ought to give them freedom. We ought to give them liberty. We ought to give them their rights. But we treat them as incompetent wards."

While a number of Indian leaders were offended by portions of his remarks, most agreed that James had accurately assessed the situation. No one challenged the truth of it. But many, including the press, resented him for stating that truth. The statement and its publicity made the plight of American Indians a topic of national discussion. It just so happened that the National Congress of American Indians had scheduled their annual meeting this same week in Washington.

I reached over and patted James on the knee. He was quietly looking out his window, and now he turned and covered my hand with his. "How did your talk go this morning?" I asked. Because of all the furor, James had made a surprise visit to the Indian Congress, speaking in place of Ken Smith, his Assistant Secretary for Indian Affairs.

"I told them that if my words caused hurt, I apologize for that. But I did not apologize for my message. The Indian people have been abused by the U.S. Government for too many years, and we've got to bring about change."

"How can you change it?"

"The only way it can be done is if Indian leaders will take their message to Congress. I can't change the laws and treaties. Only Congress can."

"This morning when I prayed for you, I asked that these Indian leaders would accept the truth, even if it was painful."

James nodded, then rested his head on the back of the seat. My interest in the Indian people began during my childhood on the Wyoming plains. When my children were small I would read them Indian stories—not the cowboy-and-Indian type, but stories about their way of life and culture, and about their heroes, such as Crazy Horse and Chief Joseph.

It hurt to see that so few people cared about their plight today. On many reservations unemployment was astronomical, often as high as 80 percent. Some of their living conditions were primitive. They were not even allowed to run their own schools and thus provide an education that might improve the chances of their children. Yet not one Congressman or Senator had risen up in defense of the Indians during this conflict. Media criticism of James ignored the fact that he was the first Interior Secretary to appoint a reservation Indian—Ken Smith—as Assistant Secretary for Indian Affairs. James was told that he was the first Interior Secretary to visit the Navajo reservation, the nation's largest, and address their Congress. He was the first Secretary to visit the second-largest tribe, the Cherokee Indian Nation. With Ken Smith, he had helped formulate President Reagan's Indian policy, which encouraged tribal self-government and a move away from direct federal control of reservations.

As our car pulled into the driveway of the Senate Office Building, I prayed again that James and I would be able to encourage these Indian leaders and their wives. *Lord, help us to say the right things. Help them to understand that, though they've been hurt, they need to take advantage of this fresh public awareness of their plight.*

The room was crowded with 250 to 300 tribal leaders and their wives, representing most of the nations in the United States. A few of them were wearing native dress, but most of the men wore suits. A few suit-wearers also wore wide-brim felt hats. In front, some presentations were being made from a floor microphone, but no one seemed to pay close attention. In the middle of the room was a large table filled with hors d'oeuvres. Usually in such a setting I followed my husband as he mingled with the crowd. But tonight I felt that it was important for me to launch out on my own so that together we might possibly meet everyone.

James began immediately, introducing himself to a group of men near the door. I chuckled as I watched him stick out his hand and announce, "Hi, I'm Jim Watt." Several times I had said to him, "People know who you are. You don't have to tell them your name." But James continued to do it, for he found it difficult to assume that people would recognize him.

On one side of the room I saw a number of women sitting in a row of chairs against the wall. Many sat with stony faces, staring straight ahead, saying nothing. The only signs of movement were their eyes, strong and piercing, sizing up all who entered the room. I put out my hand to the first woman in the row: "I'm Mrs. Watt, the Secretary's wife." She looked up at me in amazement, and a little smile turned her lips. "It's good to meet you," she answered cordially.

Slowly I worked my way up the row toward the front of the room, introducing myself to each woman. The farther I went, the easier it became. At the end of the row a small group of women stood talking, and I introduced myself to them. One of them said, "I've got a problem." Her voice was abrupt, inviting me to prove I really cared. I asked her if there were something I could do for her. "We're not getting the right health care on our reservation. The pharmacist isn't giving us the medicine we are supposed to get."

"That doesn't sound right to me. Have you written a letter of complaint?"

"Yes, we've complained about it for years. Nothing's been done about it."

"Would you please send a letter to me in care of my husband's office? When I get the letter, I'll make sure it gets to the right person so you get the help you need. The government funds are there to help you, and this man is apparently mismanaging them." (This woman did write to me and I was able to see that her problem was solved.)

Pleased with my work so far, I now headed into the center of the room, where most of the men were congregated. As I approached the first group I was unsure of protocol and decided to wait to see if they offered to shake my hand.

The first man I met wore long braids and a felt hat. He gave me a stern look. "Your husband hurt our feelings with what he said. We don't want our reservations abolished."

I smiled, thankful that I knew the facts. "You haven't

listened to my husband. Did you hear what he said to you this morning?"

A sly grin came over his face. "I listened. I just wanted to see what you would say." We both laughed and shook hands, then he motioned for me to follow him. "I want to introduce you to some other leaders."

One after another, I was introduced to the tribal chiefs. Most of them were very kind and extended their hands in greeting. "It's a good thing your husband came today," said one.

We headed toward two men standing apart from a larger group, and when they saw us coming, one of the men immediately folded his arms tightly across the top of his chest. I was introduced to them, the chief and his executive assistant from a tribe in the Pacific Northwest. The chief, his arms remaining folded, stared straight ahead and refused to look down at me. *Oh, Father, please soften this man's heart,* I said in a quick prayer. Then I shook hands with the executive assistant and offered my hand to the chief. He ignored me and said nothing.

"I'm very pleased to meet you," I said with a pat on his folded arms. "I'm glad you could come to this meeting in Washington." Standing erect and immobile like a statue, the chief didn't even acknowledge that he had heard me. A surprising stubbornness welled up within me, and I was determined to at least have him acknowledge my presence. All the other chiefs had shaken my hand; why wouldn't he?

I turned to the chief's assistant and asked, "What was your response to my husband's speech this morning?"

"We were not pleased," he said sternly. "The children on our reservation attend a public school. The children in the school accuse our children of having venereal disease."

The chief's body stiffened with those words, and one

look at his face revealed his anger. My husband's comments, meant to expose their plight, had also caused this tribe great pain. I could understand why the chief was so angry. "That would hurt so deeply," I said quietly. Though my voice didn't crack, I could feel emotion tugging at my throat. "I can understand why you would be so disappointed. If someone accused my children of having venereal disease, it would hurt me, too."

The chief dropped his head and looked at me. For a moment I stared into his black-brown eyes and no longer saw anger, but pain from years of racial abuse and misunderstanding. He dropped his arms and spoke very softly, but with great authority: "I will call home and tell my family to accept the Secretary's apology."

"Thank you. That is really most gracious of you. I would understand if you couldn't do that. My husband did not mean to hurt you. He wanted to call attention to your plight on the reservations."

The chief nodded and turned away. He did not shake my hand, but I knew that we had touched hearts. The man who was introducing me around the room touched my elbow and whispered, "You did a good job. That will go a long way. I'm going to tell your husband that you did a good job."

Just then James was introduced at the floor microphone, and the entire room—that had ignored numerous other announcements and introductions—suddenly became so still you could have heard a feather fall. I had to stand on my tiptoes to see James' head in the front corner. He spoke briefly, boldly reiterating what he had already said this morning.

"I want to say again that if my words have caused you hurt, I apologize for that hurt. But I do not apologize for my message because the Indian people of America have been abused by the U.S. government for too many years. I've given you an opportunity. Don't muff it. I've taken abuse of the press, and some of your people have attacked my motives. But one thing it did do—it got attention. Your people deserve a chance. They deserve an opportunity. The problems are severe. I'm willing to address them with you. I'm not willing to address them without you." I was surprised by their hearty applause when James finished speaking.

That was a special moment for me. As we rode home, I thought again how proud I was to be James Watt's wife. In the face of abuse, he hadn't backed down from his message. His motive was right. He had addressed the real issues. While some didn't appreciate facing the truth, others did, and I prayed that our efforts together that evening would be a step toward a real solution.

• • •

Not all my attempts at helping my husband were as successful as the experience with the Indians. One evening we attended the National Chamber of Commerce dinner where, among the 2000 in attendance, James was one of the guests of honor. Here, as at so many of the formal dinners, James and the other officials were given individual introductions. The applause for each member was polite. But when James' name was announced, an eruption of applause swelled through the room.

Lately I had noted that hearing applause for James was not enough to quiet a rumbling of discontent within me. It seemed that some who said they supported James' policies only cheered in the banquet rooms. Those who opposed him used the media channels, the streets, and the mailboxes. I could not shake the fact that our name was being smeared.

And I had my own reputation to think about. I had

stopped using charge cards with my husband's name imprinted, to avoid comments by sales clerks on the horrors of James Watt. I didn't need that. Did my name always have to be linked with his controversies? I felt guilty when I avoided being recognized in order to escape snide remarks, but why couldn't I enjoy the applause, now, for his name?

We were seated at the head table on either side of the new chairman of the board of the Chamber of Commerce. While James talked with the chairman, I enjoyed a chatty conversation with the president of the Chamber on my left. He shared with me how just that day the Chamber had used their business network to defend James' policies.

As we waited for the main course, I could hear James explaining to his host some of the frustration he had endured because environmental groups tried to stifle business expansion. I could tell that James was having a difficult time convincing the man of his problem, and rather than focusing on my own discussion, I kept an ear tuned into the conversation to my right.

"One thing I don't understand," James said, "is why businesses are helping fund special-interest groups that turn right around and fight the private-enterprise system."

"Oh, I disagree," the chairman said. "All you've got is a public relations problem. Those groups aren't as bad as you think."

"You haven't tried to start or expand a new business. Do you realize that there have been no new coal leases issued in the United States for the last 15 years? Not only is our energy future at stake, but this means thousands of jobs."

Aware that I was being rude, I struggled to turn my attention back to the president of the Chamber, who was showing me great courtesy. But it was impossible to carry on one conversation while eavesdropping on another. I could feel frustration rising within me. For two years my husband had had his name raked through the mud by the press. Almost everything he said was misinterpreted or twisted. Now here was a man who ought to understand what James was trying to do, but he didn't.

"Jim, you just need to hire a good public relations man to create a new image for yourself."

That does it! I couldn't listen to this anymore. I put my hand on the chairman's arm. When he didn't notice me, I increased the pressure until he finally turned and faced me. With a trembling voice I told him, "I am sick and tired of having our name smeared across this nation. My husband's name is thought to be a bad word in every household. Even the school kids are being taught that James Watt is a terrible man. You businessmen just think of public relations. It's a battlefield. What are you doing to help? Do you think my husband can fight alone for jobs?"

Suddenly I realized that everyone at the table was quiet and staring at me. One look at my husband's face told me I'd blown it. James never defended himself personally, and he did not want me to do so either. *O Lord, what have I done!* It was one thing to express my feelings at home to my husband. But never had I revealed myself this way in public. The chairman broke the tension and gently patted my hand and said, "That's okay, Honey. Everything's going to be all right." Then everyone returned to his discussion. The chairman's wife, sitting opposite me, leaned over and said, "I understand. But it surely isn't as bad as you think it is."

Again the anger swelled within, but this time I kept my peace. I knew it *was* as bad as I perceived. But rather than react to her, I said, "Please forgive me. It was wrong for me to speak like that." I asked each person at the table to forgive me while privately concluding that they just didn't understand our pressures.

The evening entertainment, featuring Marie Osmond, started shortly thereafter. We had already informed our hosts that we would have to leave early. So when the lights were lowered, it was a relief to slip out of that room and into the sanctuary of our official car. "James, I'm sorry," I said as soon as Ralph closed our door. "That was rude. Please forgive me. I'm sorry I embarrassed you."

James put his arm around me. "That's all right." As far as he was concerned, it was over.

My husband's forgiveness did not relieve my inner turmoil. That night, lying in bed, I prayed, *Lord, please forgive me. I was wrong to explode like that.* But a nagging uneasiness had me in its grip, and the next day I still couldn't shake that feeling. At the Bible study for Cabinet wives, I told them what had happened and asked them to show me why I wasn't feeling God's forgiveness. One of the wives, whose husband had also been ridiculed in the paper, leaned over and gave me a strong pat on the knee. "Honey, you defend your husband any way you can!" Everyone laughed, including me, but it didn't help my problem. The anxiety remained.

The next morning, during my prayer time, I began by singing a musical prayer, asking God to expose my problem. Although I had asked for forgiveness, I still felt a heaviness. I realized now that this emotion had been building for a couple of months. I needed repentance, but what was the problem?

It didn't take long for God to answer. *Rebellion.* It became clear that I was rebelling against having a difficult pathway. I wanted a smooth, pleasant road. Surely James had suffered, but so had I. Although God had promised never to give us more than we could handle, my outburst proved that I felt James and I now had more than we could bear. I was tired of our name being constantly used in jokes and jeers. Even though God had helped us through every crisis during more than two years in Washington, I felt I had reached the end.

Lord, You're right. Repentance began by agreeing with God. *And I see how my rebellion must have hurt You. I have accused You of expecting too much of me. I have accused You of refusing to give me the help I need. Please forgive me for rebelling against You.* Now I was asking forgiveness for the right reason. In that brief moment I experienced God's peace and relief from churning anxiety. If He had called us to endure even greater problems, He also had promised to provide whatever resources we needed to persevere. *Now please strengthen me and show me how to walk beside You in the hard places.*

That evening I shared with James what God had shown me. "I'm ashamed," I told him, "that I only wanted the honor of your name. I was only concerned about myself and I was trying again to avoid conflict. Please forgive me, Honey. In every way I can, I want to take your name."

James seemed a little surprised by my confession. "I've never even thought about my name," he said. "But I know a name that's been mocked for about 2000 years. It's His name we want to take."

How true. Why hadn't I thought of that? The intense abuse James had received was nothing in comparison to the fact that God's name has been insulted and misunderstood for centuries. Where is it today that Jesus Christ is not mocked and scorned? His name has even become a swear word.

The banner in the stairwell took on new meaning for me. James used that as a daily reminder that he was dedicated to serving the President. But it was also a reminder to me that God would provide me with whatever it takes to handle any situation.

CHAPTER TEN

RESIGNED.

James was quiet as he quickly ate breakfast. One look at his face warned me that he was weary. He had campaigned for the Republican party in New Mexico over the weekend, so that had meant two grueling weeks without any break. But it was the morning newspaper that revealed the real reason for his weariness. By a two-to-one margin the Senate had voted to place a 60-day moratorium on Interior Department coal leases. In addition, the newspaper I had saved for him had announced Iran's threat to close the Persian Gulf in their war with Iraq. And there was further unrest in Latin America.

"You have an important speech this morning?" I asked.

"To the Chamber of Commerce."

"How can I pray for you?"

"I want them to see the big picture." He pointed to the newspapers. "With these conflicts around the world, as much as 50 percent of our oil supply could be cut off. Yet some members of Congress try to stifle every attempt we make to become energy self-sufficient."

"Let me know how it goes," I said as he stood up, grabbed his briefcase, and headed out the door.

He called me in midafternoon. "I think I'm in trouble."

"What do you mean?"

"Doug says my speech this morning is going to cause problems."

I felt a little knot in my stomach. "What did you say?"

"I was talking about how Congress had asked me to appoint a commission to investigate our coal-leasing program. My point was that I had followed all the rules concerning a balanced makeup of the commission. I said, 'We have every kind of mix you can have. I have three Democrats, two Republicans. I have a black, I have a woman, two Jews, and a cripple. And we have talent.'"

"Oh, James!" I groaned.

"How bad is it?"

"You said 'cripple.' The word you should have used is 'handicapped.'"

"Well, they laughed after I described the commission, like it was a joke. I didn't intend it as a joke."

"Jamie, what are you going to do?"

"I've already apologized to Dr. Gordon." (He is a distinguished coal-policy expert from Penn State University, whose arm is paralyzed.)

After we hung up, I went immediately to my prayer corner. By the time I was on my knees, the tears were flowing. Maybe it was a woman's intuition, but underneath everything else I sensed that this was the end. It would be impossible to recover. Yet I wasn't disappointed. Over and over in my mind I thought, *He's my man, Lord. He's my man. I understand him.*

It was so like James. I knew he hadn't been making a joke. This morning he was not in an entertaining mood, for he felt deeply that the future security of our country was at stake. It was his style to state the facts as he saw them, whether people liked them or not. It was a strength that helped him focus on the issues, but also a weakness. He failed many times to account for people's feelings. *Glub, glub, glub. We are going "down," and I am proud to go "down" with him.*

The next morning's *Washington Post* confirmed our fears as we saw their overblown front-page coverage of this mistake. Later in the day I read some more clips. The rest of the country wasn't too concerned at first. The *New York Times* gave it only a few inches. Associated Press didn't overplay the story, but they did report that "Gordon, who is Jewish and whose arm has been crippled since contracting polio as a child, said Watt seemed sincere in his apology to him but that he was still upset by the entire episode."

But the *Post* grabbed hold of it and wouldn't let go. *They are contacting Republican Senators and are systematically printing every negative quote they can find.* Senator Rudman of New Hampshire called James "an embarrassment to the President who appointed him, an embarrassment to the party to which I proudly belong, and an embarrassment to the country." Senator Weicker said that my husband "articulates the trash of American thought," and "what one does with trash is what I suggest the President of the United States do with James Watt." Each article was like a blow from an axe. The worst was that several Republican Senators from the West, where James had his strongest support, now turned away and demanded his resignation.

With hurt in his voice, James shared with me a phone

conversation he had with Senator Robert Dole. The Senator had chided him. "You should know that we don't use the word 'cripple' anymore. That went out with the Dark Ages. The word is now 'handicapped' or 'disabled.' "

"Senator, I never think of you as either handicapped or disabled," said James. "You're extremely capable. You just happen to have a crippled hand." The Senator, whose right arm was paralyzed in a World War II injury, laughed and seemed to understand my husband's reasoning. Then we read in the papers how the Senator called James a liability to the Republican party's Senate majority and said, "If I'd been President, he would be gone."

James quickly sent a letter of apology to President Reagan, who accepted it and publicly stated that it was a closed case. But the continuing publicity convinced James otherwise. I noticed that he was not meeting this with his characteristic optimism. Always before at the height of any controversy, James was able to charge right through it. This time he was not talkative. He was no longer thinking ahead to the future.

Friday night a horde of reporters gathered outside our home, hoping to get James to break his two-day silence. We escaped to a friend's home. "James, you're not facing this the same way as the other controversies," I said as we sat on the edge of the bed. "Tell me what's different."

"All the other flaps have been over policy. I could keep my eye on my goal and move us right through the hubbub." He was silent for a moment, staring at the floor. "This is a personal mistake. There is no defense for a personal mistake because this is an unforgiving town."

Suddenly I understood his dilemma. He had decided early in his term that he would boldly defend his men, his policies, his decisions. But he would not defend himself. Just months earlier James was criticized for appointing only qualified Republicans to a scientific commission. Repeatedly the news had carried charges that the Reagan Administration was derelict in appointing minorities.

I wanted to urge James to call a press conference, to tell why he had chosen each talented member, to admit again that he had said the wrong word. Perhaps it would make a difference. *But he has apologized, hasn't he? And it made no difference. The statement is deliberately being shortened to a drumbeat. Lord, show us what to do.*

As we climbed into bed, I asked, "What do we do now?"

"We should get the resignation letter we wrote many months ago and deliver it to the President. I'm glad we wrote it back then so that we don't have to write it in the thick of this crisis. It only needs to be typed."

The next morning we drove to his office. James planned to call Jim Baker and Ed Meese to make arrangements to deliver his letter to the President. But he was struggling with his emotions, and he didn't want to call yet. He phoned Steve Shipley and Doug Baldwin and they quickly drove to the office. "You have to call Kittie, too," I said. "She would want to type the letter."

I sat on the blue leather couch and watched James. He did not try to hide his pain from his closest friends. He had shared every other thing with them as they all had battled in the trenches during nearly three years in office. Steve and Doug were struggling to control their emotions as they reached out to support my husband. I was wrenched as I watched these strong men. It was one thing for my husband to be vulnerable with me. But now, in his characteristically open manner, he was sharing his defeat fully with the men who had respected him and had faithfully followed his charging leadership. I was overcome with choking tears and admiration.

James had always said that, when he became a liability to the President, he would gladly step aside. He told us now that this was the time. With fresh resolve he called Jim Baker and asked when he could deliver his resignation letter to the President. Baker said Reagan had a busy schedule. There was a rodeo and a special barbecue at the White House. "Let's talk about this later," he said. "Don't do anything prematurely. We'll discuss it tonight."

That didn't satisfy my husband, so he called Ed Meese at home. James explained what he wanted to do, and then listened. When he covered the phone and raised his eyebrows, I knew something surprising was taking place.

"Ed said in no uncertain terms, 'You're not going,' " reported James after hanging up. We all sat still, stunned at the news. "He said 'The President has said you're not going, and he is adamant about it. We're behind you all the way.'

"You mean they don't think this will hurt the President?" I asked.

"He said conservative leaders would be outraged. They're forgiving people . . . . unfortunately, the *Washington Post* is not so forgiving."

But there was no "hole-in-the-foot award" to help this blow over. Every day the *Washington Post* hammered James. (It was not until after his resignation that the editors admitted that there was nothing wrong with the words he used. Rather, it was the "connotations . . . and everyone knows what they were.") Whenever pressure seemed to ease, a few more quotes were added to fan the fire. One morning I hurriedly read a quote that I mistakenly attributed to Senator Dole, who had just been mentioned: "If someone is capable of doing that [using the term 'cripple'], he's probably capable of calling a black man a nigger and a Jew a kike." I thought the weight of those words would surely crush me.

It was several hours later before I discovered that it was actually violinist Itzhak Perlman who was quoted. I was ashamed to think how many times I had been unforgiving when others had misquoted James. Although we had never met, I understood how the magnificent artist Perlman could respond out of his own pain with such vehemence. We had greatly admired Perlman's virtuoso performances. But even more, James and I had admired his courage as he walked out onto the stage with arm crutches.

A Senate resolution calling for James' resignation was delayed, but Republican friends doubted they could block it for long. The *Post* reported a poll, saying that by a four-to-one margin Americans who had an opinion thought James Watt should be dismissed. Actually 43 percent said they had no opinion.

It was probably too late, but many friends were now rallying to our side. Senator John East of North Carolina, who is confined to a wheelchair, said he was not insulted by the word "cripple" and publicly backed James, as did Senators Stevens and Simpson and a few others. But most of the political leaders who tried to speak for James couldn't get their views printed or reported.

Leaders from the Council for Volunteer Americans presented 120,000 postcards and letters collected on James' behalf since spring. "The press and ecology bureaucrats have concentrated on getting Watt no matter what the cost," said group leader Bob Brostrom, who is disabled by polio. That news was reported in the

Washington Times, but not in the *Post.* Two Christian television networks urged their viewers to call in if they supported James. They received between 6000 and 8000 calls. Letters and telegrams flooded the Interior Department and the White House, urging James to stay on the job.

But James was dejected. His shoulders slumped and deep weariness clouded his face. One afternoon he came home three hours early and took a long nap, then slept ten more hours that night. On Wednesday afternoon James had received news that a U.S. District Judge had ruled against him regarding five coal leases in North Dakota. It was a constitutional issue regarding separation of powers between executive and legislative branches of government. "That judge just overturned 200 years of constitutional law," said James, shaking his head.

The next morning there were three articles concerning James in the *Post*—two on the front page—plus two columns, 12 letters to the editor, and of course an editorial cartoon. *O Lord, all this because James didn't say "handicapped."* Kneeling on the living room carpet with the articles before me, I wept, and didn't even try to stop the tears from splashing onto the newsprint. Former President Gerald Ford had said that James had become a burden to Reagan. Republican Senator Charles Percy said that James had "a duty, an obligation, a responsibility. . . . to at least put a letter of resignation on the President's desk." I knew it was hopeless when I read James Kilpatrick's column. The conservative writer wrote a touching column: "Watt is by no means the monster he has been made to appear. . . . He has been a good steward." But he too felt that this was the end. "So long, Jim, it's been good to know you."

After a long week at the office, James came home

early on Friday. Some friends had offered the use of their farm, an hour's drive north of Washington, so James could escape. He slipped into a red flannel shirt, heavy camel-colored pants, and black boots. The dark, drizzly weather reflected his mood as I drove out of Washington. I reached over and laid my hand on his knee, just to let him know I was with him. Usually he responded to my tenderness and affection. But now there was no response. He was distant. He didn't talk. There was no optimistic "We're-going-to-lick-this" attitude. At the farm he seemed unable to concentrate on anything, even a television program or a book.

It became apparent that James was experiencing depression. The symptoms were there—passiveness, loss of interest, hopelessness, withdrawal, inability to concentrate. He was sleeping far more than normal. He was emotionally, intellectually, and physically exhausted. There was no fight left in him. Three years of constant abuse had taken their toll.

Realizing his depression, I wanted to be even closer to him. If only it were possible to get inside him and experience all he was feeling. I didn't try to cheer him up with a false enthusiasm, which would only have been detrimental. Instead I tried to get him to express his feelings. It was difficult, and often he chose not to respond. I tried to cheer him by reminding him that we had planned a vacation in sunny California in a few days. There it would be warm and he could escape the pressure of Washington. Concentrating on his hurt kept me from becoming discouraged myself. He needed me to stay next to him and be strong emotionally.

On Sunday James was more encouraged following a session of private prayer, where he felt an assurance that he would be led through it all. Together we focused on several verses of Scripture. For the next few days it seemed that every verse on the Moravian Daily Text spoke to our situation.

"The lowly shall once again rejoice in the Lord" (Isaiah 29:19 NEV).

"Seek first His kingdom and His righteousness, and all these things shall be added to you" (Matthew 6:33 NASB).

"He leads me in the paths of righteousness for His name's sake" (Psalm 23:3 KJV).

The morning of October 5 we were scheduled to fly to Santa Barbara to spend ten days on our friend Tom Barrack's ranch. The Scripture that morning was, "The Lord lifts up those who are bowed down" (Psalm 146:8 NIV). James had breakfast with Ed Meese before we left, and he told the presidential counselor he needed to resign. Ed again encouraged James to wait, and if it didn't blow over, then he could resign when he returned home.

James said little on our cross-country flight. He had tried twice to resign, and had been rebuffed. I knew that when he made a decision he felt was right, he was frustrated when he couldn't act on it. Emotionally he couldn't handle this for much longer without a resolution. With gentleness, I showed him the book I'd been reading about recognizing the normal symptoms of depression. We joked together about his being in the "sixth stage." I was relieved, and so was he, now that we knew what to expect in this letdown.

I was sitting next to the window as we landed in Santa Barbara. It was a beautiful, clear sunny day and for a moment my spirits lifted. Then as we taxied toward the gate I saw a huge swarm of local press. We were used to media surrounding us wherever we traveled publicly. But this was a private vacation. I wondered how they learned what airline we were flying.

James, his face set firm, said nothing.

As soon as the cabin door was opened, a chipper airport official came aboard and asked James if he would like to give an interview. "No," he said, shaking his head. "Then your car is waiting for you," she replied, and left the plane. No one made any effort to disperse the mob at the base of the ramp.

For a moment I wished we had had a couple of security personnel from the Department to accompany us. James had insisted that this be a private trip at our own expense. We had no choice but to plow through the mob alone.

At the base of the stairs several microphones were shoved in James' face. Reporters were rudely yelling at him for a comment. We were pushed and shoved by reporters jockeying for better position as we tried to fight our way through. A woman immediately in front of me held a long boom mike within inches of my husband's face so he couldn't move without being hit in the mouth. I reached over and grabbed the microphone to jerk it away. We finally broke through the mob, and Tom was waving us to the refuge of his car. James succeeded in not saying one word to the press through the ordeal.

As we started to move, we noticed that many of the reporters were already in their cars, ready to follow us. With squealing tires, Tom pulled out of the loading zone, wove between a couple of cars toward the airport exit, and entered the southbound freeway. Half a mile down the road, with the chase cars closing in on us, Tom made a fast U-turn onto the northbound lanes and ditched the press.

James was laughing now. "Way to go, Tom. This is just like the movies!"

"Welcome to California," said Tom with a smile as we slowed down to 55 and relaxed for the 40-mile drive to his ranch in the Santa Ynez Mountains. James stretched out his legs and looked out the window, enjoying the scenery. Suddenly he stiffened. "My gosh, Tom, the press is chasing us with a helicopter!" I noticed Tom's eyebrows rise. He was probably thinking the pressure had gotten to James more than he realized. Then the helicopter came closer and dipped toward us, and we recognized that it was from Channel 3, KEYT. Tom turned off the highway onto a gravel road and headed into the hills, finally stopping underneath a grove of trees. The helicopter hovered over us for a few minutes and called in a chase car. We were followed all the way to the ranch.

Even at the ranch we could not escape the press. They camped outside the gate. On a hill overlooking the property, they trained their telephoto lenses on us. James found this demeaning. He wanted to escape from the gawking eyes of the media. "At least they're respecting the property rights," he said. "The national press corps wouldn't have done even that."

The quarter-horse ranch was sprawled out in a beautiful setting. All the buildings were in the same low, white stucco style with red-tiled roofs. There were several stables with roses beside each door, and a dozen stalls by a corral used to train cutting horses. We stayed in a guest house decorated with large pieces of California wicker. At noon on Friday we walked down that half-mile path to the main ranch house where the Barracks lived. Beautiful live oak trees and a dry riverbed lined one side of the road at the base of the Santa Ynez Mountains. In the distance we could see the mountain where President Reagan's ranch was located.

"It sure clears my mind to be here," James said. "To hear the bawling calves at night, and the smell of the animals. The sunshine. Riding horses."

But James was still not relaxing. "Lani, I can't take this much more. We need to get this over with." He was talking again about resigning.

"You don't want to wait until we get back to Washington?"

"What good would that do? It's not going to go away. The Senate will almost certainly bring up the resolution for a vote."

"But the President doesn't have to accept it. He's the only one who has authority to release a Cabinet officer, and he's backing you fully."

"I simply can't handle a vote. I'm spent. We've done all we set out to do in the Department. It's time to go. Our usefulness has expired."

We walked silently for a few moments, then I put my arm around his waist. "I'm with you all the way."

We lingered over lunch with Tom and Christie Barrack, and James told them of his decision. "I'd really like to get it out of the way so we can enjoy the rest of our time here." He looked up toward the hill where he knew the photographers were staked out.

Suddenly I thought of all the press at the entrance to the ranch. They had waited patiently for two days. "If you're sure you cannot politically survive, then why don't we saddle up the horses and ride down to the camp where the media are located and announce that you're resigning. Then we can ride off into the sunset! That's just how John Wayne would have done it!"

James rocked back in his chair and laughed, and the Barracks joined in. "That's it!" James laughed. "Let's do it." With that decision I could see the cloud of depression lift.

After lunch James called Ed Meese and made the arrangements. The announcement was scheduled for Sunday afternoon in order to minimize coverage in the weekly news magazines that went to press earlier in the weekend. We laughed when we also decided that it would be wise to wait until all the weekend football games were over so no great play would be missed. Kittie was instructed to deliver the letter to Ed Meese on Sunday, and Steve Shipley and Doug Baldwin were asked to fly out and join us.

"I know just the place to stage this," said Tom. He pointed out a large live oak tree at the base of the ranch, near the gate. Some Texas longhorns were grazing nearby. "I'll put some extra feed underneath that tree. You ride up between that tree and the press, and they'll be able to get some terrific pictures."

James' spirits were lifted by the fact that he would be able to orchestrate this announcement. Rather than facing the antagonistic horde of newspeople in Washington, and then being hounded for comments until we escaped the city, we could do it in a friendlier setting. He would go out with Western dignity. Tom went down to the press camp and suggested that there might be a rodeo on Sunday afternoon. Since "they'd been so considerate, James would ride down and visit" with them for a few minutes.

On Saturday James talked again with Ed Meese to confirm that he really intended to go through with his decision. Then he left me to go play tennis, and the reality of his decision began to hit me like a punch in the stomach. I let the tears come, wishing James were there to hold me. I wanted him to be near me at this moment. But it was better to let him go and receive the comfort I needed by talking to God.

I thought about the Cabinet wives who would probably schedule a farewell party, as we had done for other wives who left. Each one had received a beautiful gold medallion with her husband's tenure on one side and "Cabinet Wives" on the other. It seemed to me it was a medal of honor I could wear with pride.

I thought fondly of the encouragement I had received. Susan Baker had called and prayed with me. Betty Ruth Bell had twice called and asked us not to resign. Cathy Donovan had reminded me of something I had told her when her husband was under attack. "You said, 'Tell Ray that the good he has done is written in indelible ink. No one will be able to remove it.' " She was encouraging me that what my husband had done, that was good for America, would not be erased.

Sallie Clingman had asked me point-blank, the same day this controversy had erupted, if I were disappointed with James and what he had said. I shared with her how well I knew him, and that his humanness did not disappoint me. "Sallie, you've walked with me through all the controversy of these past three years. You know how true it is that conflict brings out the worst in me, because it brings out what is already there. But today I can tell you that conflict also brings out the best in me. The Lord has made me a winner!"

One day I had received a call from Rosemary Tribble. "Do you remember the letter you sent me when my husband was running for the Senate?" Her husband had been attacked in the press for some of his high moral convictions. "Your letter to me is worn on the edges and stained with tears because so many times—not just during the campaign, but since then— I've needed what you wrote. Now I'd like to read it to you."

I hadn't remembered what I had written, but as she began reading, the words touched me deeply. I choked up again now as I thought of them:

Dear [Leilani].
You've been on my heart for several days and I knew you'd like to know that prayers and sunshine thoughts

are beaming your way. . . . If you can keep on choosing to stay in the front line, please know that many are praying for strength for you as a wife and as a mother and as a woman of destiny in this hour of America's determination. May you be known in your household . . . as a devoted woman, one who knows that investing in the life of others is worth the pain and sacrifice which are required to do it. Nothing beats fulfillment of opportunities you have. . . . May God abundantly supply tears when you need a good steadying cry, laughter when you need comic relief, sleep sufficient for your health, though the hours are short, and multiplied joy in your sacrifice. Without Him, this day wouldn't be, nor would this challenge be yours.

Fondly,

[Rosemary Tribble]

Lord, thank You for helping me. For strengthening me. For being a Father who comforts and cares. I love You.

My mind quieted, and I sat gazing out into the beautiful mountains to the east. My tears were therapeutic, my remembrances encouraging. There was no despair or discouragement at this moment. *Glub, glub, glub. That's funny, Lord. If our boat is capsizing, why don't I feel as if I am drowning? Where is all the panic I feared?* I realized that our boat did not represent our circumstances, but our relationship. I saw our little boat being scooped up on a wave and thrust out into smooth water, away from the storm. *Where are we headed now?* I wondered. Words that had been a gift from the Sisters of Mary rang like a sweet sounding bell in my mind: "How God will help us, I do not know. But that He will help us, I do know."

I called our children during these quiet moments to share with them the resignation plans. Their fierce pride in their father made our words come slowly. It was hard being apart during this crisis, unable to hold each other. Perhaps that was the hardest part.

Sunday dawned as bright and sunny as the other days had been. Because of the distraction the media would have created, we could not attend church, as was our usual visiting custom. So we watched a television service instead. After a relaxing morning, the excitement began to build. At the appointed time we gathered in the Barrack Ranch office with Tom and Christie, and Steve and Doug.

James dialed the President.

I couldn't sit, but paced back and forth, praying. My palms were wet, and I felt a lump in the middle of my throat. *Lord, please strengthen James right now. His loyalty has been so deep. He's given a chunk of himself to this cause. Please keep him strong in these moments.*

The President knew why James was calling and did most of the talking. Once during the ten-minute conversation James raised his eyebrows and pointed to me. I stopped pacing. "Thank you, Mr. President. Yes, she has been marvelous through all of this. Stronger than I have been." It was all I could do not to cry—to think that the President would think of me at a time like this.

James had taken some notes during the conversation, and after it was over, he told us what President Reagan had said. "He was very supportive. He said that I'd taken a lot of abuse and that no one should have to take that. It reminded him of a quote attributed to Franklin D. Roosevelt, who was talking about the resignation of one of his high officials. He said, 'He did what had to be done, and in doing it he stepped on some toes and is big enough to admit it and move on.'" James stopped to savor this moment he'd had with the President and our close friends in the room. Then he added, "We talked about the lynch mob. The Senate and the press had simply become a lynch mob. He said the only

way to deal with a lynch mob is to get out of their
road and move on, so you can live to fight another
day."

Now it was time to make the announcement. We
changed clothes, mounted our horses, and rode down
to meet the press. We giggled like kids as we rode over
the crest and saw the throng of waiting reporters. I was
surprised at my calmness. There were no butterflies now.
We arrived at the agreed-upon spot, and James dismounted and helped me off my horse. We could hear
the clicks and the whining motor drives of the cameras,
but no one asked any questions. James clipped a microphone to his shirt, then pulled his resignation letter out
of his pocket. A murmur from the crowd indicated to
me that they suddenly realized the significance of this
moment. Holding the reins of the horses, who were con-
tent to eat the grass, I looked up at James as he started
to read the letter, and felt a rush of pride:

> Dear Mr. President:
> The time has come.
>
> At my confirmation hearing in January of 1981, I
> outlined the major changes we knew were needed in
> the management of our natural resources if we were
> to restore America's greatness. With your undaunted
> support, those changes have been put in place.
>
> We confronted the neglect and problems. We gave
> purpose and direction to the management of our na-
> tion's natural resources.
>
> The restoration of our national parks, refuges and
> public lands is well under way. In fact, all the Depart-
> ment of Interior lands are better managed under our
> stewardship than they were when we inherited our
> responsibility.
>
> Our actions to reduce the Nation's dependency on
> foreign sources of energy and strategic minerals are
> working.
>
> Balance is being restored.
>
> It is time for a new phase of management—one to

consolidate the gains we have made. It is my view that my usefulness to you in this administration has come to an end. A different type of leadership at the Department of Interior will best serve you and the nation.

I leave behind people and programs—a legacy that will aid America in the decades ahead. Our people and their dedication will keep America moving and in the right direction.

It has been a high honor to serve the Nation under your leadership. You are the right man for America. My wife, Leilani, and I will continue to support you with our prayers and in any other way you may ask.

With this letter, I ask permission to be relieved of my duties as Secretary of the Interior as soon as a successor is confirmed.

Sincerely yours,
Jim

After he finished reading, he looked up as he folded the letter and put it back into his pocket. "Now I'm going to mount my horse, and then I will take questions." He laughed and said, "'If there is any question I don't want to answer, or I don't like, I can just ride off and that will be the end of it."

Everyone laughed. They waited as James helped me back on my horse, then mounted his.

"Do you have any ideas who will succeed you?"

"No, that is up to the President."

"Did you discuss any potential candidates?"

"No."

"Mr. Secretary, what are your immediate plans?"

"I think I'll stay here at the ranch until I get my batteries recharged . . . or until Tom runs me out!"

"What about after you leave office?"

"I appreciate the question because I need to file a classified ad: 'Looking for work.' " The reporters laughed. "Seriously, we'll be doing several things. We will continue our crusade and our efforts to establish spiritual freedom and political liberty in this country, for that is the real battleground."

James talked to the press for about ten minutes, and finally said, "Thank you. I've enjoyed this time." Then we turned our horses as if to ride off into the sunset.

Back at the ranch we dismounted at the corral, and as soon as my feet hit the ground, my legs turned to jelly. "James, do you know the last time I rode a horse? I've just been figuring it out. It was 30 years ago!" To the last detail, the announcement had been successful. There was laughter and praise and hugs all around.

It was over.

In a short while we would gather at the ranch house to watch the home video of the announcement, filmed by the ranch manager. As the others began the walk down the lane, James took my hand and prayed, "Father, thank You for defending us these past years, and for giving us protection and provision through this trial. You led us through it, just as You said You would. We look forward to the future You have for us."

As we slowly walked toward our cottage, I thought again of the President's encouraging words to James: "Move on so you can live to fight another day."

THE WHITE HOUSE

November 8, 1983

Dear Jim:

It is with great regret that I accept your
resignation as Secretary of the Interior,
effective at noon on November 8, 1983.

I believe that history will call you one of
our very best Secretaries of the Interior.
You took office intending to be a wise steward
of our natural resources, and you have succeeded
in that mission. Our nation needs both wilderness areas, faithfully preserved, and appropriate resource development, carefully planned
to protect the environment. You have understood
the need to balance these two goals and have done
so with dedication and success.

I know you also in another role, as a deeply
compassionate Christian who has offered leadership to millions of Americans who want to see
traditional values exemplified by their national
leaders. I am certain that you will continue to
offer our nation inspiring moral leadership for
many years to come.

Finally, Nancy and I know you and Leilani as
good friends, and we send you our warmest best
wishes for every future happiness.

Sincerely,

Ron

The Honorable James G. Watt
Secretary of the Interior
Washington, D.C. 20240

CHAPTER ELEVEN

BETTER THAN ALL YOUR PLANNING

O utside, the bitterly cold weather was unusual for Tulsa, yet it added to the Christmas spirit in our daughter's home. Erin was continuing many of our family traditions, including the Christmas tree decorations—the tiny white twinkle lights, white paper angels, and beautiful ribbons. The tree occupied one corner of the living room. At the bottom branches were two wooden angels for 13-month-old baby Joel.

On a bookcase near the tree stood six little trees I had cut out of green construction paper. Written within the fold of each one was an inspirational thought I hoped would summarize our Christmas discussion, which had become a Watt family tradition. These trees were reminders of God's message to me several months earlier, when I had struggled with the misunderstanding surrounding the Beach Boys crisis. *Wait. It will be better than all your planning.* At the time, I had rummaged through the boxes in our basement to find the story from which that meaningful phrase had come.

When I had found it, I sat in the stairwell devouring the children's booklet, *God's Trees*. My indignation had melted into wonder as I grasped the lesson of each tree: To have purpose was worth the pain of preparation. It had been many years since I had shared that story with my family, but I had decided then to read it again this Christmas.

The family gathered in the living room. We had already enjoyed an evening of turkey and homemade bread, Joel's love and antics, and laughter as we opened brightly wrapped packages. It had been two months since James' resignation. Just being together was what we needed.

We were dressed in our warm sweaters and James sat next to me. Erin and her husband, Terry, were on the couch. Eric and his fiancee, Becky, completed our intimate circle. Erin asked, "Dad, what's the discussion topic for tonight?"

"Well, I've been thinking about how easy it is to miss the significance of the disruptions in our lives." For the next few minutes we talked about how we respond to upheaval and interrupted goals. We laughed as we shared some of our own experiences. We agreed that, because of our own plans, we often fail to understand God's intervention in our lives.

"Talk about missing the significance of something," I said. "Because of all the media attention on the choice of music, I had almost wished that this year the Fourth of July would go away. As it turned out, God was going to use that evening to proclaim His majesty. More than 300,000 people came out on that rainy day to hear the inspirational and patriotic music on the Washington Mall. The number of people who needed medical care was one-tenth that of the previous year and there were no reported injuries from broken bottles or drug overdoses as in the past."

Erin and Terry Blain with Joel, Leilani and James, Becky and Eric Watt

I shared with them how the nearly 800 guests—families of the Department employees and staff of various Senators and Congressmen who served on Interior committees—had watched the spectacular fireworks from the roof and balconies of the Department of the Interior. "Showers of multicolored sparklers rained over the Washington Monument. Explosions of light shook the sky. But in the distance an even more spectacular light show was taking place. Huge bolts of lightning, many flashing horizontally, lit up the horizon. With every heavenly display, the crowd gave increasing applause.

"When the show was over, your Dad and I visited with the people as they left. Many remarked on the fireworks-lightning show. 'God must have thought you did a good job, Jim,' one said. 'He gave the best show.' Another commented, 'God's fireworks were the best.'

"I agreed with them. It had been a patriotic day, but God's fireworks had outshined ours. It was a graphic reminder that nothing happens to us that God can't turn into something good. Do you remember the story, *God's Trees*,* that I used to read to you at Christmas? I found it a few months ago when God was assuring me that His plans are always better than my own. It begins...

"Far away, on a hillside, grew a forest of trees," I began. "The trees were very happy with life just as it was. But sometimes they spoke of the future, of the things they would like to do and be when they grew up.

"In this forest there was a mother tree and her three little trees. One tree said, 'I should like to be a baby's cradle. I think a baby is the sweetest thing I have ever seen, and I should like to be made into a baby's bed.'

*God's Trees. Used by permission of Child Evangelism Fellowship, Inc. Warrenton, Missouri 63383.

"A second tree spoke. 'That would not please me at all. I want to be something important. I should like to be a great ship, strong and stately. I should like to cross many waters and carry cargoes of gold.'

"A third little tree stood off by himself and did not speak. 'What would you like to be?' asked Mother Tree. 'Have you no dreams for the future?'

"'No dream,' he answered, 'except to stand on this hillside and point men to God. What could a tree do better than that?'

"Years passed, and the little trees grew tall and beautiful. One day men came to the forest and cut down the first tree. 'I wonder whether I shall be made into a baby's cradle now,' he thought. But the little tree was not made into a cradle. Instead, it was hewn into rough pieces and carelessly put together to form a manger in a stable in Bethlehem. He was heartbroken. 'This is not what I planned,' he wailed, 'to have cattle eating out of me.'

"But God, who loves little trees, whispered to him, 'Wait. I will show you something.' And He did! For on a cold, still night, Mary and Joseph came to that stable, and there she gave birth to the son of God—Jesus— and laid Him in that manger. 'This is wonderful,' whispered the tree. 'In all my dreams I never thought to hold a baby like this. This *is* better than all my planning. I'm part of a miracle.'

"Months passed, and men came again to the forest to cut down the second tree. 'I wonder whether I shall be made into a great vessel now and do great things,' he thought. But instead he became a tiny fishing boat, owned by a simple Galilean fisherman named Peter. The little boat was most unhappy. 'To think that my life has come to this. Just an old smelly fishing boat. And Peter not a very good fisherman!'

"But God, who loves little trees, said to him, 'Wait.

I will show you something.' And He did. One day, from out of the crowd, came a person named Jesus. He sat in the boat and taught the crowd beautiful words of wisdom. Then He told Peter to launch out into the deep and let his nets down. There were so many fish that the net broke. The little boat trembled, not so much from the weight of the fish as with the weight of wonder in his heart. 'In all my dreams I never thought to carry a cargo like this! Why, I'm part of a miracle. This *is* better than all my planning.'

"Weeks went by and one day men came to the forest to cut down the third tree, the one who wanted to just stand on a hill and point men to God. He was most unhappy as the axe cut into his bark. 'I don't want to go into the valley,' he cried. 'Why couldn't men leave me alone!' The men tore away the branches and cut deeper into his very heart. They hewed it apart, then put it together again in the form of a rude cross. 'This is terrible. They are going to kill someone on me. I never wanted this to happen; I only wanted to point men to God,' he wailed.

"But God, who loves little trees, said to him, 'Wait. I will show you something.' And He did. A few days later, a great multitude gathered outside Jerusalem. In their midst was Jesus, carrying the cross. When they came to the place called Calvary, they nailed Him to that cross and crucified Him. The cross shuddered beneath the weight of agony and shame. But then a miracle happened.

"Jesus, when He had cried with a loud voice, gave up His life. And the earth quaked and the rocks trembled. When the centurion saw these things, he was afraid and said, 'Truly this man was the Son of God.'

"Then the little tree that had become a cross remembered the echo of a past promise from heaven: 'And I, if I be lifted up from the earth, will draw all men unto Me.' The tree began to understand. 'This is wonderful,' he thought. 'I am part of a miracle. In all my dreams I never thought to point men to God in this way. This *is* better than all my planning.' And so it was. For hundreds of trees stood on the hill slopes through the years, but not one of them has reconciled men to God."

No one spoke when I finished reading. Each of us pondered the meaning for himself. At the end of the worn booklet I had written in pencil, "Lord, take our lives and do what You will. That will be better than all our planning." The date by those words read "December 1970." It was now Christmas 1983, and I could see how God's plans had proved better than mine.

For years my plan was to avoid conflict at all cost. God's plan was to place me in the most intense conflict and demonstrate His power to take me through it.

My plan was to change any circumstance that made me uncomfortable. God's plan was to change me so I could experience peace and contentment in the midst of the worst situation.

My plan was to pursue my own desires and ignore my husband's career. God's plan was to put me in James' boat so I might experience all of his fears, as well as his triumphs.

My plan was to become an influential Bible teacher. God's plan was for me to be an intercessor, praying primarily for James.

My plan was to resist being dominated by James. God's plan was for me to appreciate him for who he is, to deal with all his strengths, and to love him with all his weaknesses.

My plan was to avoid suffering, and to choose only those parts of the Christian life that were comfortable. God's plan was for me to experience so much love that I could endure the public and private pain with

James and glimpse the meaning of standing beside Christ.

I looked around the room at the faces of my family and realized they were as touched as I had been. I knew then that we had all been thinking about the past 13 years. We could see how God had turned every difficult circumstance into triumph.

But what about this one? My husband had been out of office nearly two months now. What would the future hold?

Quietly we each moved to the bookcase to take our green paper tree from the shelf. The inspirational thought written within became a symbol of our expectation and prayer for the new year: "Lord, make of my life whatever pleases You."

I reached out for my husband's hand. Only our thoughts passed between us. God had a continuing plan for our lives. That I knew. I did not understand what it might be, but I had confidence in God's guidance. I could rejoice with these very special words: *Wait. I will show you something.* He has. And He will.

It will be better than all your planning.

PHOTO CREDITS:

Cover photo: Courtesy Fredde Lieberman, *Charisma* Magazine
p. 47 Alan Markfield/Gamma-Liaison
p. 68 Rick Browne/Picture Group, Inc.
p. 79 Department of the Interior/Public Affairs Photo
p. 101 Karl Schumacher/The White House
p. 115 Department of the Interior/Public Affairs Photo
p. 119 Department of the Interior/Public Affairs Photo
p. 133 Bill Clark/National Park Service
p. 139 Gary Ambrose/*The Los Angeles Times*
p. 147 Mary Ann Fackelman/The White House
p. 178 Bob Ponce/*Santa Barbara News-Press*
p. 183 Pete Souza/The White House
p. 186 Dorothea F. Heit

Social Style Concepts referenced on page 144 were adapted by Don Thoren, The Thoren Group, Tempe, Arizona 85283 for the "Interpersonal Effectiveness Seminars," from original research by Personnel Predictions & Research (PPR), a Division of The TRACOM Corporation, Denver, Colorado 80206.